SRA

Corrective Reading

► # Comprehension Skills

Enrichment Blackline Masters   **Comprehension B2**

W9-CNN-823

Siegfried Engelmann • *Susan Hanner*

SRA McGraw-Hill

Columbus, Ohio

A Division of The McGraw-Hill Companies

SRA/McGraw-Hill

A Division of The McGraw·Hill Companies

Copyright © 2001 by SRA/McGraw-Hill.

Printed in the United States of America.

Send all inquiries to:
SRA/McGraw-Hill
8787 Orion Place
Columbus, OH 43240-4027

ISBN 0-02-674814-2

3 4 5 6 7 8 9 0 MAL 05 04 03 02 01

Table of Contents

Part 1

Underline the common part. Circle each sentence that tells **why.** Combine the sentences with **because.**

1. The telephone did not work.

   The telephone was broken.

   _____

   _____

2. Sam drank milk.

   Milk is good for him.

   _____

   _____

3. She is riding her bike.

   She has no car.

   _____

   _____

4. Jeff has a cavity.

   Jeff will have to go to the dentist.

   _____

   _____

Part 2

Circle the subject and underline the predicate in each sentence.

1. The leaves are turning red, orange, and yellow.

2. We watched the toddler cross the room.

3. The digestive system changes food to fuel.

4. That book has many chapters.

5. Months have passed since she has been home.

6. Cars, buses, and trains are methods of transportation.

Part 3

The _____ tubes branch off into smaller and smaller tubes.

      artery   capillary   bronchial

1. Cross out the word that completes the sentence correctly.

2. Circle the nouns in the sentence.

3. Above the first noun, write the name of the body system the sentence discusses.

4. Underline the verb in the sentence.

Writing sentences, conventions of grammar, vocabulary/following directions
Directions: If necessary, read the directions for each part. When students have completed the page, present each item and the answer. Correct any errors.

Part 4

Underline the common part. Fill in the circle beside the word that combines the sentences correctly. Combine the sentences with that word.

1. Dan likes to play soccer.

Alex likes to play soccer.

◯ and   ◯ who   ◯ which

_____

_____

2. Nancy likes her bedroom.

Her bedroom is painted pink.

◯ and   ◯ who   ◯ which

_____

_____

3. The boat belongs to Bill.

Bill gave me a ride.

◯ and   ◯ who   ◯ which

_____

_____

Part 5

Fill in each blank.

1. _____

2. _____

3. _____

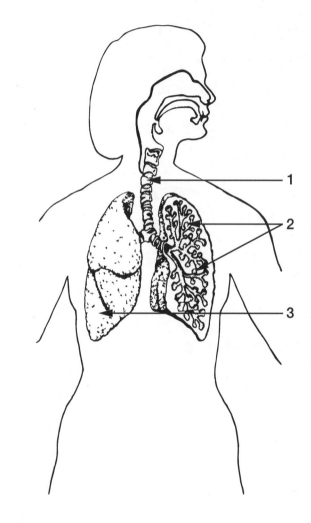

Conventions of grammar/writing, graphic aids
Directions: If necessary, read the directions for each part. When students have completed the page, present each item and the answer. Correct any errors.

Part 1

Underline the nouns. Draw a line **over** the adjectives. Circle the verbs.

1. The woman worked in a small office.

2. A body has many organs.

3. People like national parks.

4. The respiratory system brings oxygen to the blood.

Part 2

Complete the instructions.

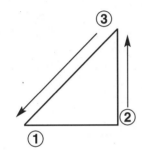

1. Draw a _____

   _____ .

2. Draw a _____ line _____

   from the _____ end of the

   _____ line.

3. Draw a _____ line from the

   _____ of the _____

   _____ to the _____

   _____ of the _____

   _____ .

Part 3

Circle the subject and underline the predicate of each sentence.

1. Dogs, cats, and hamsters can all be pets.

2. My brother David plays tennis.

3. Playing basketball can be fun.

4. The trachea and bronchial tubes are part of the respiratory system.

Part 4

Write a word that comes from **reside** or **produce** in each blank. Then fill in the circle beside **verb, noun,** or **adjective.**

1. Our _____ is a brick house.

   ◯ verb   ◯ noun   ◯ adjective

2. The movie _____ took ten months.

   ◯ verb   ◯ noun   ◯ adjective

3. Did he _____ in that house when

   he was young?

   ◯ verb   ◯ noun   ◯ adjective

4. It was a _____

   meeting.

   ◯ verb   ◯ noun   ◯ adjective

Conventions of grammar, following directions, inflectional and derivational suffixes
Directions: If necessary, read the directions for each part. When students have completed the page, present each item and the answer. Correct any errors.

Part 5

Read the passage and answer the questions.
Circle **W** after each question that is answered
by words in the sentences, and underline those
words.
Circle **D** after each question that is answered by
a deduction.

> **Your respiratory system brings oxygen
> into contact with your blood. The air
> goes into your bronchial tubes. Then the
> air goes into capillaries, which soak up
> oxygen.**

1. What system brings oxygen to your blood?

_____

_____ **W   D**

2. Where does the air go? _____

_____ **W   D**

3. What do the capillaries do? _____

_____ **W   D**

4. Is the blood in the capillaries red or dark?

_____ **W   D**

Part 6

Underline the common part. Fill in the circle
beside the word that combines the sentences
correctly. Then combine the sentences with that
word.

1. Los Angeles is on the West Coast.

Oregon is on the West Coast.

◯ and   ◯ who   ◯ which

_____

_____

2. Martha baked cookies.

The cookies had chocolate chips.

◯ and   ◯ who   ◯ which

_____

_____

3. Oxygen is a gas in the air.

Capillaries soak up oxygen.

◯ and   ◯ who   ◯ which

_____

_____

4. Sam watched his father.

His father was a baseball player.

◯ and   ◯ who   ◯ which

_____

_____

Deductions, conventions of grammar/writing sentences
Directions: If necessary, read the directions for each part. When students have completed the page, present each item and
the answer. Correct any errors.

4

Part 1

Tell how the things are the same.

1. My hands were like ice.

_____

_____

2. His muscles were like rocks.

_____

_____

3. The sun looked like a red ball.

_____

_____

4. Barb's eyes were like saucers.

_____

_____

Part 2

Write **R** for each fact that is **relevant** to what happened. Write **I** for each fact that is **irrelevant** to what happened.

The firefighter put out the fire.

1. The firefighter was old. _____

2. The firefighter used a hose. _____

3. The fire was in the attic. _____

4. The firefighter was named Donna. _____

Part 3

Fill in each blank.

1. _____

2. _____

3. _____

4. _____

5. _____

6. _____

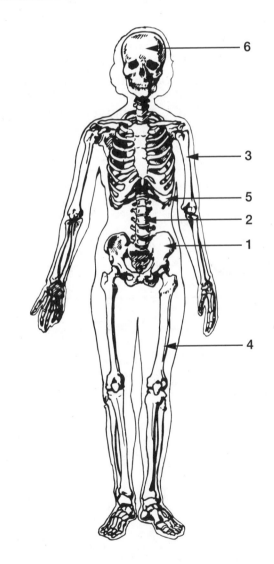

Comparisons/figurative language, main idea/relevant and irrelevant details, graphic aids
Directions: If necessary, read the directions for each part. When students have completed the page, present each item and the answer. Correct any errors.

Part 4

Circle the subject and underline the predicate in each sentence.

1. Pens and pencils are writing tools.

2. Swimming alone can be dangerous.

3. The circulatory system moves blood in your body.

4. Baking a wedding cake takes skill.

5. Newspapers have lots of sections.

☆ Part 5

Imagine you are going to the grocery store. Put the following foods in the correct groups.

Shopping List: milk, hamburger, green beans, apples, eggs, potatoes, bacon, bananas

Fruits: _____

_____

Meats: _____

_____

Vegetables: _____

_____

Dairy: _____

_____

Part 6

Underline the common part. Combine the sentences with **who, which,** or **and.**

1. That mail carrier always walked to work.

   That mail carrier was a young man.

   _____

   _____

2. Marcia likes to read about horses.

   Marcia rides every day.

   _____

   _____

3. The zookeeper liked his job.

   His job was exciting.

   _____

   _____

4. David has a new computer.

   David has a new desk.

   _____

   _____

Conventions of grammar, classifying, conventions of grammar/writing sentences
Directions: If necessary, read the directions for each part. When students have completed the page, present each item and the answer. Correct any errors.

Part 1

For each word on the left, write the letter of its definition on the right.

1. trapezius   _____
2. biceps   _____
3. produce   _____
4. abdominal muscle   _____
5. triceps   _____
6. gastrocnemius   _____
7. quadriceps   _____
8. selection   _____
9. criticize   _____
10. regulatory   _____

a. (n.) the muscle that goes from the ribs to the pelvis
b. (n.) the muscle that covers the front of the femur
c. (n.) the muscle that covers the back of the lower leg
d. (n.) the muscle that covers the back of the neck
e. (n.) the muscle that covers the front of the humerus
f. (v.) make
g. (n.) something that is selected
h. (a.) that something regulates
i. (v.) find fault with
j. (n.) the muscle that covers the back of the humerus

Part 2

Circle the subject and underline the predicate in each sentence.

1. The pulmonary artery is a large artery in your body.
2. Kathy smiled at her little sister.
3. To make cider is hard work.
4. The heart pumps the blood.
5. Dad walks the dog every morning.
6. Swimming is good exercise.

☆ Part 3

Fill in the circle next to the item that does **not** fit in each category.

1. Things to eat with
   ○ plate   ○ fork   ○ shoes
2. Things to listen to
   ○ radio   ○ pie   ○ television
3. Things to cut with
   ○ scissors   ○ lawnmower   ○ comb

Definitions, conventions of grammar, classifying
Directions: If necessary, read the directions for each part. When students have completed the page, present each item and the answer. Correct any errors.

Part 4

Tell how the things are the same.

1. Jim eats like a bear.

_____

_____

2. I slept like a log last night.

_____

_____

3. The flowers were like a bone.

_____

_____

Part 5

Write a word that comes from **modify** in each blank. Then fill in the circle beside **verb, noun,** or **adjective.**

1. The _____ hot rod won the race.

  ◯ verb   ◯ noun   ◯ adjective

2. Did you _____ the window frame?

  ◯ verb   ◯ noun   ◯ adjective

3. They made a lot of _____

to the building.

  ◯ verb   ◯ noun   ◯ adjective

Part 6

Fill in each blank.

1. _____

2. _____

3. _____

4. _____

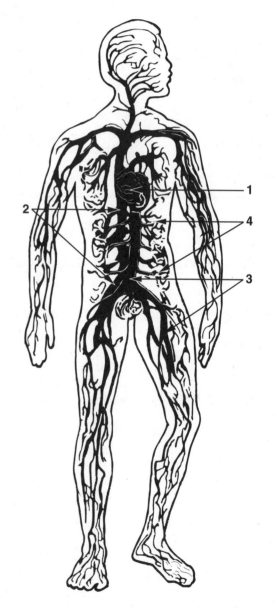

Comparisons/figurative language, inflectional and derivational suffixes, graphic aids
Directions: If necessary, read the directions for each part. When students have completed the page, present each item and the answer. Correct any errors.

Part 1

Underline the common part.
If one of the sentences tells **why,** combine the sentences with **because.**
If neither of the sentences tells why, combine the sentences with **who, which,** or **and.**

1. Jill got good grades.

Jill worked hard.

_____

_____

2. Brad saw Kim.

Kim rode her bike fast.

_____

_____

3. Bob got a new shirt.

Bob got a new hat.

_____

_____

4. Lane needed a haircut.

Lane went to the barbershop.

_____

_____

5. The race started at ten in the morning.

I was tired after the race.

_____

_____

Part 2

Tell how the things are the same.

1. Her smile is like sunshine.

_____

_____

2. The cake was like a rock.

_____

_____

3. John's feet were like blocks of ice.

_____

_____

Part 3

Circle the subject and underline the predicate in each sentence.

1. Babysitting can be a big responsibility.

2. To win a game is exciting.

3. **Triceps, selections,** and **biceps** are nouns.

4. The bike and lawnmower needed to be repaired.

5. The pulmonary artery carries carbon dioxide.

Conventions of grammar/writing sentences, comparisons/figurative language, conventions of grammar
Directions: If necessary, read the directions for each part. When students have completed the page, present each item and the answer. Correct any errors.

Part 4

Write a word that comes from **modify** in each blank. Then fill in the circle beside **verb, noun,** or **adjective.**

1. They drive a _____ van.

   ○ verb   ○ noun   ○ adjective

2. They _____ the van late last year.

   ○ verb   ○ noun   ○ adjective

3. We will be _____ our house in the fall.

   ○ verb   ○ noun   ○ adjective

4. We plan to make a few _____ to the first floor.

   ○ verb   ○ noun   ○ adjective

Part 5

Underline the nouns.
Draw a line **over** the adjectives.
Circle the verbs.

1. Pam raced her older brother.

2. They both wore new green sneakers.

3. Pam tripped on a large rock.

4. Her brother slipped on a banana peel.

5. They started the race again.

☆ Part 6

Read the list of things. Decide how you could classify or categorize them into smaller, related groups.

football	tennis racket	basketball
wagon	toy cars	dolls

1. What categories could you use?

   _____

   _____

2. What things would you place in each category?

   _____

   _____

   _____

Inflectional and derivational suffixes, conventions of grammar, classifying
Directions: If necessary, read the directions for each part. When students have completed the page, present each item and the answer. Correct any errors.

LESSON 6

Name _____

Part 1

Underline the nouns. Draw a line over the adjectives. Circle the verbs.

1. The weather is cold and rainy.

2. The car was moving in the mud.

3. Two small boys ran down the hill.

4. Every student should have a pencil.

Part 2

The _____ artery carries

dark blood to the lungs.

1. Finish the sentence.

2. Circle the adjectives.

3. Above the second noun write the name of the body system the sentence is talking about.

4. Below the verb, write the verb that means **controls.**

Part 3

Fill in each blank.

1. _____

2. _____

3. _____

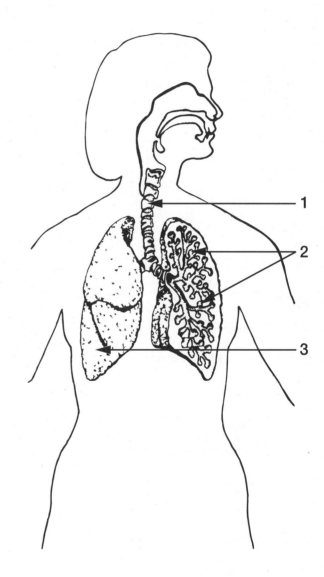

Conventions of grammar, vocabulary,/following directions graphic aids
Directions: If necessary, read the directions for each part. When students have completed the page, present each item and the answer. Correct any errors.

☆ Part 4

> **A compound word is made by joining two words.**

Write the compound word made by joining each pair of words.

1. earth + quake = _____

2. sun + set = _____

3. water + color = _____

4. star + fish = _____

5. snow + ball = _____

6. egg + shell = _____

7. watch + dog = _____

8. air + plane = _____

Part 5

Tell how things are the same.

1. I ate like a pig yesterday.

_____

_____

2. Her voice is like a bell.

_____

_____

Part 6

Write **R** for each fact that is relevant to what happened. Write **I** for each fact that is irrelevant to what happened.

> **Thomas likes pizza and ice cream.**

1. Thomas has a younger sister. _____

2. Thomas needs to lose weight. _____

3. Thomas has a part time job. _____

4. His pants don't fit. _____

5. His mom is a good cook. _____

Compound words, comparisons/figurative language, main idea/relevant details.
Directions: If necessary, read the directions for each part. When students have completed the page, present each item and the answer. Correct any errors.

Part 1

Tell **two** ways that the things compared are **not** the same. Tell **one** way that the things compared **are** the **same.**

The cat cried like a baby.

1. A cat is not _____

_____.

2. A baby is not _____

_____.

3. _____

_____.

Part 2

Write a word that comes from **predict** or **modify** in each blank. Then fill in the circle beside **verb, noun,** or **adjective.**

1. He _____ the snowstorm.

◯ verb   ◯ noun   ◯ adjective

2. They plan to _____

the garage.

◯ verb   ◯ noun   ◯ adjective

3. My _____ came true.

◯ verb   ◯ noun   ◯ adjective

Part 3

Complete the instructions.

②
conclusion
① _____
digest
③
④

1. Draw a _____ _____ .

2. Draw a _____

_____ at the _____

end of line 1.

3. To the _____ of the _____

line, write the _____ that comes

from the verb _____ .

4. Write the word _____ _____

the _____ line.

Comparisons/figurative language, inflectional and derivational suffixes, following directions.
Directions: If necessary, read the directions for each part. When students have completed the page, present each item and the answer. Correct any errors.

Part 4

Read the story and answer the questions. Circle the **W** if the question is answered by words in the story, and underline those words. Circle the **D** if the question is answered by a deduction.

> A construction worker worked from seven in the morning until four in the afternoon. He had an accident at his job and cut his foot. He couldn't see the cut because his foot was bleeding so much. The blood was bright red. Putting a bandage on the cut did not stop the bleeding. He decided he needed to get help fast.

1. What color is the blood in the arteries of your foot? _____ **W D**

2. What color is the blood in the veins of your foot? _____ **W D**

3. Why is the blood in your veins almost black? _____ **W D**

   _____

4. Was the worker bleeding from a vein or an artery? _____ **W D**

5. Could the accident have occurred at nine in the evening?

   _____ **W D**

6. Did the bandage on the cut stop the bleeding?

   _____ **W D**

☆ Part 5

Make compound words from the words in the box and write them on the lines below.

thanks	mark	foot	weed
ball	book	giving	sea

1. _____

2. _____

3. _____

4. _____

Deductions, compound words

Directions: If necessary, read the directions for each part. When students have completed the page, present each item and the answer. Correct any errors.

Part 1

In each blank, write the word that has the same meaning as the word or words under the blank.

1. The _____ of the book was a
   (end)

   surprise.

2. Carla's _____ was not a good one.
   (choice)

3. The doctor _____ her teeth.
   (looked at)

4. A bicycle helmet _____ your head.
   (guards)

5. _____ to your science
   (Changes)

   experiment are needed.

Part 2

Circle the subject and underline the predicate in each sentence.

1. Nouns name persons, places, and things.

2. Every person's nervous system is made up of nerves.

3. To scuba dive takes a lot of instruction.

4. Baking bread is time-consuming.

5. All arteries carry blood away from the heart.

6. Lizards and alligators are reptiles.

Part 3

Underline the common part. Then combine the sentences with **who** or **which**.

1. Gretchen is a doctor.

   Gretchen speaks French.

   _____

   _____

2. Your heart is in your chest.

   Your heart acts as a pump.

   _____

   _____

3. Todd has a new brother.

   Todd lives next door.

   _____

   _____

4. Nerves are everywhere in the body.

   Nerves carry messages.

   _____

   _____

Vocabulary, conventions of grammar, writing sentences
Directions: If necessary, read the directions for each part. When students have completed the page, present each item and the answer. Correct any errors.

☆ Part 4

Draw a line from one word in the first column
to one word in the second column to make a
compound word. Use each word only once.

1. note   plane

2. news   cake

3. cup   book

4. paint   boat

5. air   bow

6. rain   brush

7. sail   paper

Part 5

Tell **two** ways that the things compared are **not**
alike. Tell **one** way that the things compared **are**
alike.

| The loaf of bread was like a rock. |

1. _____

   _____

2. _____

   _____

3. _____

   _____

Part 6

Read the passage and answer the questions.
Circle **W** if the question is answered by words
in the story, and underline those words. Circle **D**
if the question is answered by a deduction.

> Blood that carries carbon dioxide is
> almost black. Blood that carries oxygen
> is red. However, when you cut yourself,
> the blood is mixed with oxygen in the air.
> All blood exposed to air is red.

1. What color is blood that carries oxygen?
   _____ **W** **D**

2. What color is blood that carries carbon
   dioxide?
   _____ **W** **D**

3. What color will blood turn if it is exposed to
   air? _____ **W** **D**

Compound words, comparisons/figurative language, deductions
Directions: If necessary, read the directions for each part. When students have completed the page, present each item and
the answer. Correct any errors.

Name _____

Part 1

For each word on the left, write the letter of its definition on the right.

1. oxygen _____

2. constructive _____

3. carbon dioxide _____

4. predictable _____

5. verb _____

6. obtain _____

7. regulatory _____

8. modify _____

9. noun _____

10. adjective _____

a. (v.) get

b. (a.) something that regulates

c. (n.) a word that comes before a noun and tells about the noun

d. (n.) a gas that burning things need

e. (v.) change

f. (a.) something that is easy to predict

g. (n.) a word that tells the action that things do

h. (a.) something that is helpful

i. (n.) a gas that burning things produce

j. (n.) a word that names a person, place, or thing

Part 2

Write a word that comes from **digest** or **conclude** in each blank. Then fill in the circle beside **verb, noun,** or **adjective.**

1. What _____ can you come to about the book?

○ verb   ○ noun   ○ adjective

2. The stomach is part of the _____ system.

○ verb   ○ noun   ○ adjective

Part 3

Follow the directions.

1. Draw a horizontal line.

2. Draw a line that slants down to the right from the right end of the horizontal line.

3. Draw a curve to represent a muscle that covers the bottom of the horizontal line and attaches to the top end of the slanted line.

4. Circle the line that will move when the muscle pulls.

Definitions, inflectional and derivational suffixes, following directions
Directions: If necessary, read the directions for each part. When students have completed the page, present each item and the answer. Correct any errors.

☆ Part 4

Use the homophones from the box to complete the sentences below.

ate	cent	there	blue
eight	sent	their	blew

1. The wind _____ my hat off.

2. I _____ my breakfast early today.

3. Your backpack is over _____.

4. We _____ the package to Chicago.

5. My neighbor has _____ kittens.

6. A penny is one _____.

7. Is _____ house made of brick?

8. The weather forecast is for _____ skies.

Part 5

Circle the subject and underline the predicate in each sentence.

1. **Cold, big,** and **old** are adjectives.

2. Bike riding is good exercise.

3. Making friends is part of going to school.

4. The respiratory system brings oxygen to your lungs.

5. Oxygen and carbon dioxide are gases.

Part 6

Write **brain, nerves,** or **spinal cord** in each blank.

1. _____

2. _____

3. _____

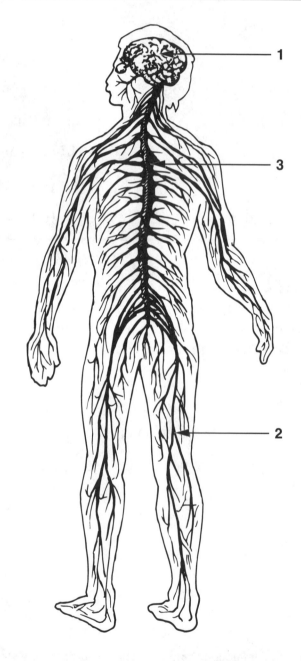

Homophones, conventions of grammar, graphic aids
Directions: If necessary, read the directions for each part. When students have completed the page, present each item and the answer. Correct any errors.

Part 1

On the lines below, rewrite the paragraph by combining the sentences that are joined with an underline. If one of the sentences tells **why,** combine the sentences with **because.**

Betsy was moving to another state. Betsy had three brothers. Her dad got a new job. Her dad is a policeman. Betsy was not happy. She will miss her friends.

_____

_____

_____

_____

_____

_____

_____

☆ Part 2

Use these homophones to complete the sentences.

pale	pail	so	sew
nose	knows	hair	hare

1. She _____ what she wants to eat.

2. His _____ tells him that breakfast is ready.

3. Bobby put sand in the _____.

4. The sick child looked _____.

5. The _____ hopped away.

6. He combed his _____.

7. Dad feels _____ happy.

8. He can _____ buttons on his shirt.

Writing/conventions of grammar, homophones
Directions: If necessary, read the directions for each part. When students have completed the page, present each item and the answer. Correct any errors.

Part 3

Tell **two** ways that the things compared are **not** the same. Tell **one** way that the things compared **are** the same.

> **She eats like a bird.**

1. _____

_____

_____

2. _____

_____

_____

3. _____

_____

Part 4

Shade in each tube that carries dark blood. Tell if each tube is a vein or an artery.

1. _____

2. _____

3. _____

4. _____

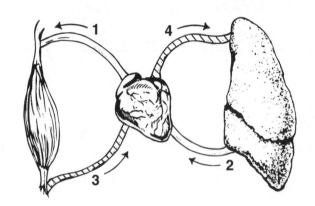

Comparisons/figurative language, graphic aids
Directions: If necessary, read the directions for each part. When students have completed the page, present each item and the answer. Correct any errors.

LESSON 11

☆ Part 1

Fill in the circle next to the correct homophone.

1. The shoe _____ was over yesterday.

   ○ sail   ○ sale

2. _____ home is for sale.

   ○ Hour   ○ Our

3. A _____ is a kind of fruit.

   ○ pair   ○ pear

4. The _____ looked ready to eat.

   ○ meat   ○ meet

Part 2

Tell which fact each statement relates to.

1. **Blood that carries oxygen is red.**

2. **Blood that carries carbon dioxide is dark.**

   a. It goes from the heart to the muscles. _____

   b. It goes from the muscles to the heart. _____

   c. It is pumped by the heart to all parts

      of the body.   _____

Part 3

Write a word that comes from **reside** or **produce** in each blank. Then fill in the circle beside **verb, noun,** or **adjective.**

1. The company stopped _____.

   ○ **verb**   ○ **noun**   ○ **adjective**

2. He _____ in an old farmhouse.

   ○ **verb**   ○ **noun**   ○ **adjective**

3. The White House is the _____ of the president.

   ○ **verb**   ○ **noun**   ○ **adjective**

4. Gary has had a _____ year growing corn.

   ○ **verb**   ○ **noun**   ○ **adjective**

Part 4

Tell **two** ways that the things compared are **not** the same.
Tell **one** way that the things compared **are** the same.

Sarah says she feels like a million bucks.

1. _____

   _____

2. _____

   _____

3. _____

   _____

Homophones, contradictions, vocabulary, comparisons/figurative language
Directions: If necessary, read the directions for each part. When students have completed the page, present each item and the answer. Correct any errors.

Part 5

On the lines below, rewrite the paragraph by combining the sentences that are joined with an underline. If one of the sentences tells **why**, combine the sentences with **because**.

> **The digestive system has an important job. The digestive system includes the mouth and stomach. First, your teeth act like sharp blades. The sharp blades cut the food into small bits. The stomach mixes the food with chemicals. The chemicals dissolve the food.**

_____

_____

_____

_____

_____

_____

_____

_____

Part 6

Fill in each blank.

1. _____

2. _____

3. _____

4. _____

5. _____

6. _____

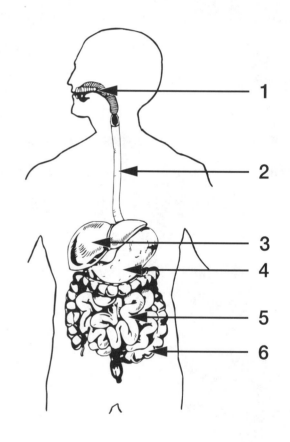

Writing/conventions of grammar, graphic aids

Directions: If necessary, read the directions for each part. When students have completed the page, present each item and the answer. Correct any errors.

Part 1

Write the instructions.

nerves _____ spinal cord

③   ①   ②

1. (what) _____

_____

2. (what and where) _____

_____

3. (what and where) _____

_____

☆ Part 2

An **antonym** is a word that means the opposite of another word. Here are some antonym pairs:

    hot/cold   in/out   up/down

Fill in the circle beside the antonym for each underlined word.

1. buy   ◯ sell   ◯ redo

2. criticize   ◯ worry   ◯ praise

3. over   ◯ under   ◯ beside

4. conclude   ◯ make   ◯ begin

5. construct   ◯ destroy   ◯ investigate

Part 3

Write **spinal cord, nerves, brain, central** or **peripheral** in each blank.

1. _____

2. _____

3. _____

1. and **2.** _____ nervous system.

3. _____ nervous system.

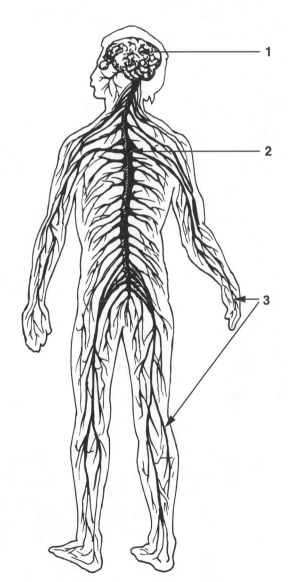

Following directions, antonyms, graphic aids

Directions: If necessary, read the directions for each part. When students have completed the page, present each item and the answer. Correct any errors.

Part 4

Read the story and answer the questions.
Circle the **W** if the question is answered by the
words in the story, and underline those words.
Circle the **D** if the question is answered by a
deduction.

> **Your brain is divided into three
> parts: the cerebrum, the cerebellum,
> and the medulla. The cerebrum helps
> you think and feel. The cerebellum
> controls your muscular system. The
> medulla controls your digestive,
> respiratory, and circulatory systems.**

1. List the three parts of your brain.

_____

_____ **W   D**

2. What is the medulla's job? _____

_____

_____ **W   D**

3. Which part of your brain works when you

feel happy? _____

_____ **W   D**

4. What does the cerebellum do?

_____

_____ **W   D**

5. Which part controls your digestive system?

_____

_____ **W   D**

Part 5

Write a word that comes from **protect** or
criticize in each blank. Then fill in the circle
beside **verb, noun,** or **adjective.**

1. The woman _____ the cashier for
making a mistake.

◯ **verb**   ◯ **noun**   ◯ **adjective**

2. The dog was very _____ of her
puppies.

◯ **verb**   ◯ **noun**   ◯ **adjective**

3. His _____ hurt her feelings.

◯ **verb**   ◯ **noun**   ◯ **adjective**

4. Some companies require their employees to

wear special _____ for their jobs.

◯ **verb**   ◯ **noun**   ◯ **adjective**

Deductions, inflectional and derivational suffixes
Directions: If necessary, read the directions for each part. When students have completed the page, present each item and
the answer. Correct any errors.

Part 1

Fill in the blank with the word that has the same meaning as the word or words under the blank.

1. The doctor _____ the cat.
         (looked at)

2. It is important to _____ the right class.
                    (choose)

3. She wants to _____ her diploma.
               (get)

Part 2

Write the instructions.   ②

         ①

                    ③ trachea

1. (what) _____

_____

2. (what and where) _____

_____

3. (what and where) _____

_____

Part 3

Circle the common part that is at the **beginning** of two sentences. Then combine those sentences with **who** or **which.**

1. The children played in the snow.

The snow lasted a long time.

The snow was good for making snowballs.

_____

_____

_____

2. His boat is thirty feet long.

His boat belonged to our grandfather.

My brother likes his sailboat.

_____

_____

3. Her teacher liked to read mysteries.

Mysteries can be scary.

Her teacher used to be a librarian.

_____

_____

4. The festival was planned for this weekend.

This weekend is a holiday weekend.

The festival has lots of food and music.

_____

_____

_____

Vocabulary, following directions, conventions of grammar/writing sentences
Directions: If necessary, read the directions for each part. When students have completed the page, present each item and the answer. Correct any errors.

25

LESSON 13

Name _____

Part 4

Underline the nouns. Draw a line **over** the adjectives. Circle the verbs.

1. Two balloons floated toward the blue sky.

2. The happy frog croaked loudly.

3. My older brother wants a new car.

4. Yesterday the class planted two pine trees.

Part 5

Shade in each tube that carries dark blood. Tell if each tube is a **vein** or an **artery**.

1.  _____

2. _____

3. _____

4. _____

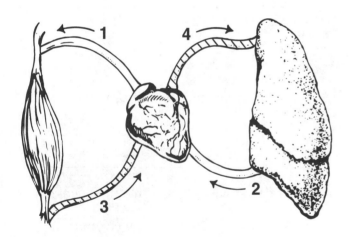

☆ Part 6

Look at each word. Choose the correct **antonym** from the box and write it in the space provided.

begin	white	open	down
thick	soft	happy	sleepy

1. hard _____

2. end _____

3. sad _____

4. up _____

5. thin _____

6. black _____

7. awake _____

8. shut _____

Conventions of grammar, graphic aids, antonyms
Directions: If necessary, read the directions for each part. When students have completed the page, present each item and the answer. Correct any errors.

Part 1

For each word on the left, write the letter of its definition on the right.

1. protective _____   a. (n.) a statement that criticizes

2. conclude _____   b. (n.) the organ that lets you think and feel

3. nerve _____   c. (v.) end or figure out

4. digestion _____   d. (n.) the body part that connects the brain to all parts of the body

5. brain _____   e. (a.) that something protects

6. production _____   f. (a.) that something is changed

7. spinal cord _____   g. (n.) the act of digesting

8. conclusive _____   h. (n.) a wire in the body that carries messages

9. criticism _____   i. (n.) something that is produced

10. modified _____   j. (a.) that something is true without any doubt

Part 2

Write the instructions

cerebrum | cerebellum

③   ①   ②

1. (what) _____

_____

2. (what and where) _____

_____

3. (what and where) _____

_____

Part 3

Circle the subject and underline the predicate in each sentence.

1. Raking leaves uses many muscles.

2. The medulla and the cerebrum are parts of the brain.

3. Carbon dioxide is a gas in the air.

4. Arteries and veins are parts of the circulatory system.

5. **Brain, nerve**, and **cerebellum** are all nouns.

6. To build a house requires much planning.

Definitions, following directions, conventions of grammar
Directions: Read the directions to each item with the student. Give the student time to respond before going to the next item. When students have completed the page, go over the items and answers. Correct any errors.

☆ Part 4

Read the sentences. Fill in the circle for the **antonym** of the **bold** word

1. The skyscraper is very **tall.**

   ◯ **short**   ◯ **hot**

2. The pancake batter was very **thick.**

   ◯ smooth   ◯ thin

3. It's easy to **go** into the city.

   ◯ stop   ◯ out

4. These cookies are **hard.**

   ◯ rough   ◯ soft

5. In the **evening** we will go for a walk.

   ◯ morning   ◯ noon

6. Do you want to go **before** the movie starts?

   ◯ after   ◯ begin

7. The **bottom** of the boat has a hole in it.

   ◯ right   ◯ top

8. Is this too **short** for you?

   ◯ sweet   ◯ long

Part 5

Write **spinal cord, nerves, brain, central** or **peripheral** in each blank.

1. _____

2. _____

3. _____

1. _____ nervous system.

2. and 3. _____ nervous system.

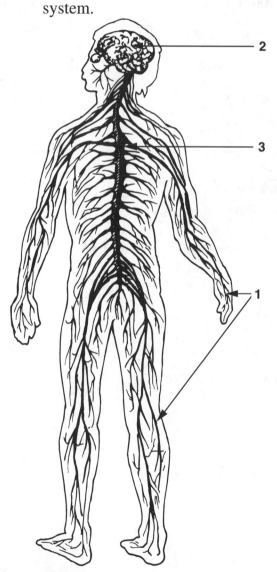

Antonyms, graphic aids

Directions: Read the directions to each item with the student. Give the student time to respond before going to the next item. When students have completed the page, go over the items and answers. Correct any errors.

Part 1

Fill in each blank

1. _____

2. _____

3. _____

4. _____

5. _____

6. _____

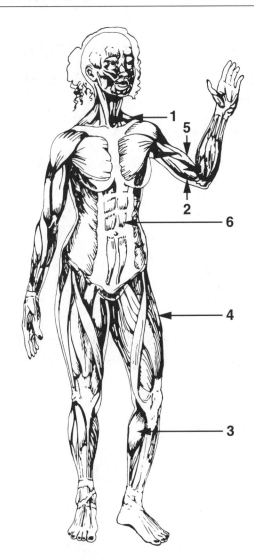

Part 2

Write the instructions.

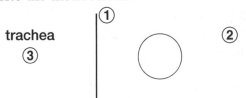

1. (what) _____

_____

2. (what and where) _____

_____

_____

3. (what and where) _____

_____

_____

Part 3

Circle the subject and underline the predicate in each sentence.

1. Nerves carry messages to all parts of the body.

2. Going to the fair is always fun.

3. My parents, brother, and sister can all drive.

4. Baseball and golf are my favorite sports.

5. Cleaning the garage is not fun.

Graphics aids, following directions, conventions of grammar
Directions: If necessary, read the directions for each part. When students have completed the page, present each item and the answer. Correct any errors.

Part 4

Underline the common part. Fill in the circle beside the word that combines the sentences correctly. Combine the sentences with that word.

1. The horse stood near the fence.

   The horse was brown and white.

   ○ **who**   ○ **because**   ○ **which**

   _____

   _____

2. The computer was broken.

   The computer didn't work.

   ○ **who**   ○ **but**   ○ **because**

   _____

   _____

3. New York is in the East.

   Maine is in the East.

   ○ **because**   ○ **and**   ○ **who**

   _____

   _____

4. Leslie was sitting on the couch.

   Her cat was sitting on the couch.

   ○ **and**   ○ **which**   ○ **because**

   _____

   _____

☆ Part 5

> • Use a **comma** (,) to separate three or more items listed together in a sentence.
> • Use a comma after the words **yes** and **no** if they begin a sentence.

Read the sentences below. Place commas where they belong.

1. You will need glue paper scissors crayons and a pencil.

2. No I didn't ask her to come with us.

3. Please bring the milk eggs orange juice and bread from the refrigerator.

4. Yes it is your turn.

5. The cooler chairs beach towels and toys need to go in the car.

6. Please pack your books homework assignment pad and pencils in your backpack.

7. We want to visit the museum zoo beach and theme park on our vacation.

8. I left my bed unmade my clothes on the floor the bathroom messy and dishes in the sink!

Conventions of grammar, commas
Directions: If necessary, read the directions for each part. When students have completed the page, present each item and the answer. Correct any errors.

LESSON 16

Name _____

Part 1

Write the instructions.

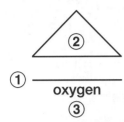

1. (what) _____

   _____

   _____

2. (what and where) _____

   _____

   _____

3. (what and where) _____

   _____

   _____

☆ Part 2

Look at the series of words or phrases in the following sentences. Decide where the commas go and add them.

1. Sandra went to the store and bought apples oranges pears and bananas.

2. On our camping trip we went fishing hiking hunting swimming and diving.

3. Before you can drive a car you have to take a class read a book on driving rules take driving lessons and pass a test.

Part 3

Rewrite each sentence by moving part of the predicate. The first item is done for you.

1. He went to sleep because he was tired.

   Because he was tired, he went to sleep.

2. Rabbits were hopping in the grass.

   _____

   _____

3. He bought a kite when he went to the store.

   _____

   _____

4. The grass is wet after it rains.

   _____

   _____

Part 4

Fill in each blank with the word that has the same meaning as the word or words under the blank.

1. A smart person _____ friends
   (chooses)

   carefully.

2. Humans _____ oxygen from the air.
   (get)

3. The man wanted to _____ the car.
   (look at)

4. The heart _____ how fast the
   (controls)

   blood flows.

Writing directions, commas, conventions of grammar, vocabulary
Directions: If necessary, read the directions for each part. When students have completed the page, present each item and the answer. Correct any errors.

Part 5

Write **R** for each fact that is **relevant** to what happened. Write **I** for each fact that is **irrelevant** to what happened.

> **Last night, Ken locked his keys in the car and had to call home for help.**

1. Ken is very tall. _____

2. Ken keeps a spare key at home. _____

3. Ken's car is pink and yellow. _____

4. Ken likes to drive. _____

Part 6

Tell **two** ways that the things compared are **not** the same.
Tell **one** way that the things compared **are** the same.

The sun is like a basketball.

1. _____

_____

2. _____

_____

3. _____

_____

Part 7

Fill in each blank.

1. _____

2. _____

3. _____

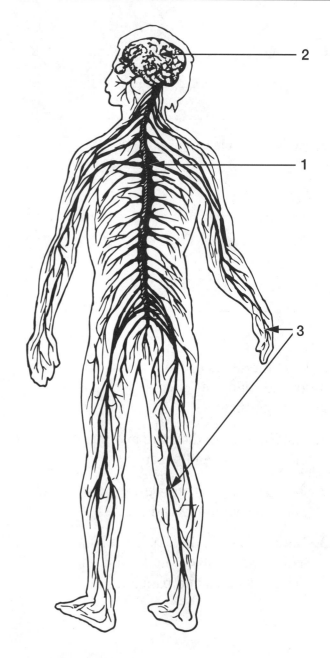

Main idea/relevant and irrelevant details, comparisons/figurative language, graphic aids
Directions: If necessary, read the directions for each part. When students have completed the page, present each item and the answer. Correct any errors.

Part 1

a. Underline the common part that is at the **end** of one sentence and the **beginning** of another. Then combine those sentences with **who** or **which.**

b. Circle the common part that is at the **beginning** of two sentences. Then combine those sentences with **who** or **which.**

1. Some animals have veins.

Some animals have bones.

Veins carry blood back to the heart.

a. _____

_____

_____

b. _____

_____

_____

2. Sense nerves carry messages to the brain.

The brain has three main parts.

Sense nerves let you feel.

a. _____

_____

_____

b. _____

_____

_____

Part 2

Fill in each blank.

1. _____

2. _____

3. _____

4. _____

5. _____

6. _____

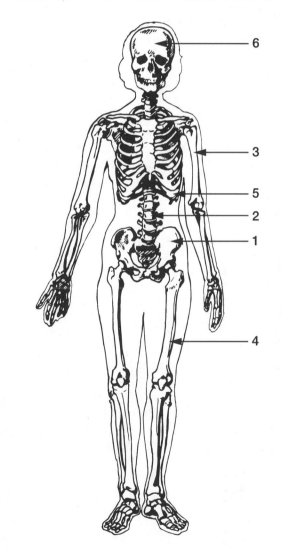

Conventions of grammar/writing sentences, graphic aids

Directions: If necessary, read the directions for each part. When students have completed the page, present each item and the answer. Correct any errors.

☆ Part 3

Read the sentences below. Place commas where they are needed.

1. Tom likes to play chess ride his bike swim and play basketball.

2. Yes please pass out the permission slips.

3. Please make your bed brush your teeth eat breakfast and walk the dog.

4. Suzi likes corn and meatloaf for dinner.

5. It's time to close your books pack your backpacks and sit down.

6. Let's go to the movies the video arcade and the park the next time we come here.

Part 4

Write a word that comes from **predict** or **regulate** in each blank. Then fill in the circle beside **verb, noun,** or **adjective.**

1. The weatherman _____ a cold winter.

   ◯ **verb**   ◯ **noun**   ◯ **adjective**

2. Her _____ that the cat would come back was correct.

   ◯ **verb**   ◯ **noun**   ◯ **adjective**

3. Your cerebellum _____ your muscular system.

   ◯ **verb**   ◯ **noun**   ◯ **adjective**

4. The end of the movie was _____.

   ◯ **verb**   ◯ **noun**   ◯ **adjective**

Commas, inflectional and derivational suffixes
Directions: If necessary, read the directions for each part. When students have completed the page, present each item and the answer. Correct any errors.

Part 1

Use the facts to fill out the form.

> **Facts:** Your name is Thomas Jones. You are twelve years old. You have an older sister named Angela and a younger brother named Jeff. Your father is a reporter and your mother is a nurse. Your address is 462 East Broad Street, Columbus, Ohio.

Instructions:

a. Enter your name on line 2.
b. Write your father's profession on line 6.
c. State your age on line 3.
d. On line 1, write your mother's job.
e. Write your address on line 4.
f. On line 5, write the sentence above that gives information you didn't use in filling out the form.

1. _____

2. _____

3. _____

4. _____

   _____

5. _____

   _____

   _____

6. _____

Part 2

a. Underline the common part that is at the **end** of one sentence and the **beginning** of another. Then combine those sentences with **who** or **which**.
b. Circle the common part that is at the **beginning** of two sentences. Then combine those sentences with **who** or **which**.

1. The woman was very tall.

   The woman was watching the football game.

   The football game lasted three hours.

   a. _____

   _____

   _____

   b. _____

   _____

   _____

2. Mars is known as the "Red Planet."

   Veronica wants to travel to Mars.

   Veronica likes movies about space travel.

   a. _____

   _____

   _____

   b. _____

   _____

   _____

Identifying facts, conventions of grammar/writing sentences
Directions: If necessary, read the directions for each part. When students have completed the page, present each item and the answer. Correct any errors.

☆ Part 3

> A **contraction** is a shortened form of two words that are joined together. When the words are joined, one or more letters are left out. An apostrophe is used to show the letters that are left out.
>
>   it's = it is   wasn't = was not

Read each pair of sentences. Circle the contraction. Underline the two words it replaces.

1. We do not know how to play.
   We don't know how to play.

2. I did not know that Brad could come.
   I didn't know that Brad could come.

3. It is supposed to be hot again tomorrow.
   It's supposed to be hot again tomorrow.

4. We will read the book after lunch.
   We'll read the book after lunch.

Part 4

Tell **two** ways that the things compared are **not** the same.
Tell **one** way that the things compared **are** the same.

The water was like a mirror.

1. _____

2. _____

3. _____

Part 5

Write the conclusion of each deduction.

1. Some planets are smaller than Saturn.
   Mercury is a planet.

   _____

   _____

2. Every brain has three parts.
   Marvin has a brain.

   _____

   _____

3. Every dog has warm blood.
   Maynard is a dog.

   _____

   _____

Part 6

Make each statement mean the same thing as the statement in the box.

> **People paid Larry to protect their residences.**

1. Larry was paid to protect people's homes.

2. People gave money to Larry for protecting their residences.

3. Larry paid people to protect their places of residence.

4. People paid Larry to guard the places where they worked.

Contractions comparisons/figurative language, forming generalizations
Directions: If necessary, read the directions for each part. When students have completed the page, present each item and the answer. Correct any errors.

Name _____

Part 1

For each of the words on the left, write the letter of its definition on the right.

1. irrelevant _____

2. conclude _____

3. nervous system _____

4. digest _____

5. relevant _____

6. examine _____

7. central nervous system _____

a. (v.) look at

b. (n.) the body system that is made up of all the nerves that lead to and from the spinal cord

c. (n.) body system that is made up of the brain and spinal cord

d. (a.) that something does not help to explain what happened

e. (v) end or figure out

f. (a.) that something helps to explain what happened

g. (v.) change food into fuel for the body

Part 2

Underline the contradiction.
Circle the statement it contradicts.

> Roger Maris, who played for the New York Yankees, broke Babe Ruth's single-season home-run record by hitting 61 home runs in one season. His record looked unbeatable. In 1998, his record was broken twice. Mark McGuire hit 70 home runs and Sammy Sosa hit 66 in the 1998 season. Batting and pitching records are always falling, but Maris's record will never be broken. Who do you think will be the next person to hit 70 home runs in a single season?

Part 3

Circle the subject and underline the predicate in each sentence. Rewrite each sentence by moving part of the predicate.

1. Dogs often bark when they are scared.

_____

_____

2. She ate a large meal at the restaurant.

_____

_____

3. The students criticized the author after reviewing her novel.

_____

_____

Definitions, identifying facts, conventions of grammar/writing sentences
Directions: If necessary, read the directions for each part. When students have completed the page, present each item and the answer. Correct any errors.

Part 4

Underline the common part. Fill in the circle beside the word that combines the sentences correctly. Combine the sentences with that word.

1. Germany is a country in Europe.

Italy is a country in Europe.

○ **which**   ○ **and**   ○ **because**

_____

_____

2. Bill wanted to skate.

Bill borrowed skates.

○ **because**   ○ **which**   ○ **but**

_____

_____

3. Cheetahs run very fast.

Cheetahs have spots.

○ **who**   ○ **because**   ○ **which**

_____

_____

4. Tammy is turning eight today.

Tammy has black hair.

○ **because**   ○ **who**   ○ **which**

_____

_____

☆ Part 5

Draw a line from the two words to the contraction.

1. I will   don't

2. she will   they'll

3. he will   it'll

4. we will   I'll

5. they will   didn't

6. it will   she'll

7. do not   we'll

8. did not   he'll

Conventions of grammar/writing sentences, contractions
Directions: If necessary, read the directions for each part. When students have completed the page, present each item and the answer. Correct any errors.

Part 1

Circle the subject and underline the predicate in each sentence. Rewrite each sentence by moving part of the predicate.

1. Your cousin broke her leg when she fell off her bike.

   _____

   _____

2. My father and brother eat cereal in the morning.

   _____

   _____

Part 2

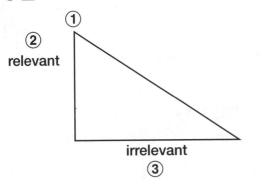

① ② relevant ③ irrelevant

1. (what) _____

   _____

2. (what and where) _____

   _____

3. (what and where) _____

   _____

Part 3

Use the facts to fill out the form.

> **Facts: Your name is Sara Jensen. You are forty-five years old. You want to buy a house. You are the president of a steel company. You make $150,000 per year. You have two children and a husband named Zeke. Your address is 154 S. Toledo Street, Pittsburgh, Pennsylvania.**

Instructions:
a. Enter your husband's name on line 2.
b. State your age on line 4.
c. On line 3, tell what you want to purchase.
d. Write your full name, last name first, on line 1.
e. Write your address on line 5.
f. On line 6, write the second sentence above that gives information you didn't use in filling out the form.

1. _____

2. _____

3. _____

4. _____

5. _____

6. _____

Conventions of grammar/writing sentences, writing instructions, identify facts
Directions: If necessary, read the directions for each part. When students have completed the page, present each item and the answer. Correct any errors.

Part 4

a. Underline the common part that is at the **end** of one sentence and the **beginning** of another. Then combine those sentences with **who** or **which.**

b. Circle the common part that is at the **beginning** of two sentences. Then combine those sentences with **who** or **which.**

1. The brain is the most complex organ in the body.
   The brain is part of the nervous system.
   The nervous system is the system of nerves in the body.

   a. _____
   _____
   _____

   b. _____
   _____
   _____

2. Sam is a zookeeper.
   A zookeeper feeds and cares for animals at a zoo.
   Sam is my older brother.

   a. _____
   _____

   b. _____
   _____

Part 5

Fill in each blank with the word that has the same meaning as the word or words under the blank.

1. The mechanic _____ his car to
   (changed)

   make the engine run quietly.

2. Carpenters _____ many different
   (build)

   types of buildings.

3. The new law is intended to _____
   (control)

   the purchase of cars from foreign countries.

4. Scoliosis is a disease that affects the

   _____.

   (body part that connects the brain to all parts of the body)

☆ Part 6

Rewrite the underlined word as a contraction.

1. There <u>is not</u> enough paper.

   _____

2. <u>It is</u> time for us to leave.

   _____

3. <u>I will</u> be leaving soon.

   _____

4. <u>Here is</u> some money for lunch.

   _____

_____

Conventions of grammar/writing sentences, context clues, contractions
Directions: If necessary, read the directions for each part. When students have completed the page, present each item and the answer. Correct any errors.

Part 1

Write **R** for each fact that is **relevant** to what happened. Write **I** for each fact that is **irrelevant** to what happened.

> **Sheryl played the trumpet in the marching band.**

1. She has blond hair. _____

2. She is twenty-four years old. _____

3. Oranges are Sheryl's favorite fruit. _____

4. She likes to march with the band. _____

Part 2

Circle the subject and underline the predicate in each sentence. Rewrite each sentence by moving part of the predicate.

1. Evan and his sister play tennis at school.

   _____

   _____

2. Tina's mother soaked her feet when she went home.

   _____

   _____

3. Mr. Marek consumed chicken in a restaurant.

   _____

   _____

Part 3

a. Underline the common part that is at the **end** of one sentence and the **beginning** of another. Then combine those sentences with **who** or **which.**

b. Circle the common part that is at the **beginning** of two sentences. Then combine those sentences with **who** or **which.**

1. Apples are good for you.
   Apples are ready to eat in the fall.
   The fall is my favorite season.

   a. _____

   _____

   _____

   b. _____

   _____

   _____

2. Henry has worked in construction for many years.
   Burt agreed to build a house with Henry.
   Burt has never built a house before.

   a. _____

   _____

   _____

   b. _____

   _____

   _____

Main idea/relevant and irrelevant details, conventions of grammar/writing sentences
Directions: If necessary, read the directions for each part. When students have completed the page, present each item and the answer. Correct any errors.

Part 4

Use the facts to fill out the form.

> **Facts:** Your name is Molly Jones. You are thirty-six years old. You are a college history teacher. You want the job of head tour guide at the Grand Canyon. Your husband is a third grade teacher. You have written many books about the Grand Canyon. Your address is 4656 Canyon Drive, Phoenix, Arizona.

Instructions:

a. State your age on line 3.
b. Write your address on line 2.
c. Write your full name, last name first, on line 1.
d. On line 6, state your current profession.
e. State the topic of the books you have written on line 5.
f. State the job you are seeking on line 7.
g. On line 4, write the sentence above that gives information you didn't use in filling out the form.

1. _____
2. _____

   _____

3. _____
4. _____

   _____

5. _____
6. _____
7. _____

   _____

☆ Part 5

> A **synonym** is a word that means almost the same thing as another word.
>
> **Examples:** small/little home/house

Use the words in the box below to write a synonym for each word.

gift	below	right	new
road	shut	single	enjoy

1. one   _____
2. present _____
3. like   _____
4. street _____
5. correct _____
6. under   _____
7. fresh   _____
8. close   _____

Identifying facts, synonyms
Directions: If necessary, read the directions for each part. When students have completed the page, present each item and the answer. Correct any errors.

Part 1

Circle the subject and underline the predicate in each sentence. Rewrite each sentence by moving part of the predicate.

1. Mary walks three miles to school every day.

_____

_____

2. Two frogs ate flies by the pond.

_____

_____

_____

3. They found a marble under the bed.

_____

_____

4. My best friend's mother saw a shooting star last night.

_____

_____

5. He reads comic books for fun.

_____

_____

☆ Part 2

Match the words in Column 1 with their **synonyms** in Column 2.

Column 1	**Column 2**
1. find	idea
2. fasten	locate
3. fearful	enjoy
4. thought	hook
5. boring	limb
6. branch	dull
7. like	scared
8. car	leave
9. close	auto
10. go	shut

Conventions of grammar/subjects and predicates, synonyms
Directions: If necessary, read the directions for each part. When students have completed the page, present each item and the answer. Correct any errors.

Part 3

Read the story and answer the questions.
Write **W** after each question that is answered by
words in the story, and underline those words.
Write **D** after each question that is answered by
a deduction.

> **Diamonds and coal are made of the
> same mineral. The mineral that
> diamonds and coal share is called
> carbon. Diamonds are used for jewelry,
> are very hard, and can cut every other
> material in the world. A diamond is
> many times more valuable than coal.
> Coal is used in industry, but it does not
> have the physical beauty of diamonds.**

1. What mineral makes diamonds and coal?

   _____

2. Jane had a piece of coal and a diamond. She
   lost one of them and was very upset. Which

   one did she lose? _____

   _____

3. Can a diamond be used to cut a piece of
   glass?

   _____

   _____

Part 4

Write **R** for each fact that is **relevant** to what
happened. Write **I** for each fact that is
irrelevant to what happened.

> **Michael bought a new pair of running
> shoes.**

1. He joined the track team.   _____

2. Michael likes to run.   _____

3. His sister does not wear shoes.   _____

4. He has red running shorts.   _____

5. Michael has outgrown his old pair
   of shoes.   _____

Part 5

This word means **an object that is changed:**

_____.

1. Cross out the words that tell what this word
   means.

2. Over the words you crossed out, print the
   word that means **that an object is changed.**

3. At the end of the sentence, print the verb this
   word comes from.

4. Circle the adjectives.

Deductions, main idea/relevant and irrelevant details, root words/following directions
Directions: If necessary, read the directions for each part. When students have completed the page, present each item and
the answer. Correct any errors.

44   © 2001 SRA/McGraw-Hill. Permission is granted to reproduce for classroom use.

Part 1

Complete the analogies.

1. Tell what part of speech each word is.

   Consumer is to _____

   as **digestion** is to _____.

2. Tell what verb each word comes from.

   Consumer is to _____

   as **digestion** is to _____.

3. Tell what ending each word has.

   Consumer is to _____

   as **digestion** is to _____.

Part 2

Follow the directions.

1. Draw a horizontal line from left to right.

2. Draw a vertical line of the same length on the right and left ends of the first line.

3. Draw a horizontal line between the two vertical lines.

4. Below the top horizontal line, write the verb that means **look at**.

Part 3

Underline the common part. Combine the contradictory sentences with **but**.
Combine the other sentences with **who** or **which**.

1. Scott cut down those trees.

   Those trees are too tall.

   _____

   _____

   _____

2. Thomas Edison invented many things.

   Thomas Edison was born in Ohio.

   _____

   _____

   _____

3. George Washington was the first president of the United States.

   The United States now consists of fifty states.

   _____

   _____

   _____

   _____

4. Gordon wanted to buy four oranges.

   Gordon bought only two oranges.

   _____

   _____

   _____

Analogies, following multistep directions, conventions of grammar/writing sentences
Directions: If necessary, read the directions for each part. When students have completed the page, present each item and the answer. Correct any errors.

☆ Part 4

Fill in the circle next to the **synonym** for each underlined word.

1. Debbie tripped and fell on the <u>trail</u>.

○ path   ○ log   ○ dirt

2. <u>Huge</u> clouds covered the sun.

○ little   ○ big   ○ dark

3. I <u>peeked</u> around the corner to see the accident.

○ jumped   ○ shouted   ○ glanced

4. She was <u>excited</u> about going in an airplane.

○ thrilled   ○ sad   ○ anxious

5. Steve <u>shut</u> the door when he went to school.

○ closed   ○ locked   ○ kicked

6. Tina <u>likes</u> corn on the cob.

○ cooks   ○ enjoys   ○ buys

7. Please <u>complete</u> your homework before dinner.

○ stop   ○ under   ○ finish

8. Do you <u>have</u> a pencil I could use?

○ own   ○ old   ○ borrow

Part 5

Underline the nouns. Draw a line **over** the adjectives. Circle the verbs.

1. Tom and Roberto are skating on the pond.

2. The man and the woman have been running for ten minutes.

3. The singers sang mostly work songs and love songs.

4. Fred hurt his little toe, and the doctor gave him a big cast.

5. His older brother consumed grapes with his lunch.

6. Her cats liked the mud.

Part 6

Make each statement mean the same thing as the statement in the box.

> Frogs and lizards consume and digest bugs.

1. Frogs and children eat insects.

2. Lizards and frogs eat snakes.

3. Lizards and frogs consume and produce insects.

4. Frogs and lizards eat bears.

Synonyms, conventions of grammar, forming generalizations

Directions: If necessary, read the directions for each part. When students have completed the page, present each item and the answer. Correct any errors.

Part 1

For each word on the left write the letter of its definition on the right.

1. obtain   _____
2. conclusive   _____
3. modification   _____
4. consumer   _____
5. motor nerve   _____
6. consumable   _____
7. sense nerve   _____
8. construction   _____

a. *(n.)* something that consumes

b. *(n.)* something that is constructed

c. *(a.)* that something can be consumed

d. *(n.)* a nerve that lets you move

e. *(n.)* a change

f. *(a.)* something that is true without any doubt

g. *(v.)* get

h. *(n.)* a nerve that lets you feel

Part 2

Underline the contradiction. Circle the statement it contradicts. Tell **why** the underlined statement contradicts the circled statement.

> In 1522, the remaining members of Ferdinand Magellan's crew arrived in Spain. Spain looked good to them. Five ships had started the trip, but only one ship returned. The crew had acquired many different spices on the journey. People in Spain paid a lot of money for the spices, since they were very rare. The king and queen of Spain were sad that only three of the ships survived the journey.

_____

_____

Part 3

Tell **two** ways that the things compared are **not** the same.
Tell **one** way that the things compared **are** the same.

> **That cupcake is like a rock.**

1. _____

_____

2. _____

_____

3. _____

_____

Definitions, identifying clues that allow one to find contradictions, comparisons/figurative language
Directions: If necessary, read the directions for each part. When students have completed the page, present each item and the answer. Correct any errors.

Part 4

Write a word that comes from **obtain** in each blank. Then fill in the circle beside **verb, noun,** or **adjective.**

1. I plan on _____ my driver's license this summer.

   ○ verb   ○ noun   ○ adjective

2. Tara _____ a newspaper from one of her friends.

   ○ verb   ○ noun   ○ adjective

3. Where did you _____ such a beautiful painting?

   ○ verb   ○ noun   ○ adjective

☆ Part 5

> **Alphabetical order** is the order of the letters in the alphabet. To put words in alphabetical order, look at the first letters of each word.

Write each set of words in alphabetical order.

a. oar   canoe   paddle

1. _____
2. _____
3. _____

b. pole   price   pump

1. _____
2. _____
3. _____

Part 6

Use the rule to answer the questions.

> **The more meat you eat, the more protein you get.**

1. Brian eats three hamburgers a day. Terry eats two hamburgers a day.

   a. Who gets more protein?

   _____

   b. How do you know?

   _____

   _____

2. Sally gets thirty grams of protein a day. Kathy gets seventy grams of protein a day.

   a. Who eats more meat?

   _____

   b. How do you know?

   _____

3. Jack eats three pounds of meat a week. Eric eats five pounds of meat a week.

   a. Who gets more protein?

   _____

   b. How do you know?

   _____

Inflectional suffixes, alphabetical order, making assumptions
Directions: If necessary, read the directions for each part. When students have completed the page, present each item and the answer. Correct any errors.

☆ Part 1

Read the words below. Number the terms in each group in alphabetical order.

1. adjectives _____

   nouns _____

   verbs _____

   adverbs _____

   pronouns _____

   apostrophes _____

   possessives _____

   tenses _____

2. capitalization _____

   punctuation _____

   abbreviations _____

   initials _____

   quotes _____

   commas _____

   closing _____

   greeting _____

Part 2

Underline the common part.
Combine the sentences with **who** or **which**.

1. Greg saw a giant apple on his desk.

   Greg has red hair.

   _____

   _____

   _____

2. The vena cava is the biggest vein in your body.

   The vena cava carries no oxygen.

   _____

   _____

   _____

3. Linda and Jim went to see a movie.

   Jim did not like the movie.

   _____

   _____

4. Misty was sad.

   Misty got her hair cut.

   _____

   _____

   _____

Alphabetical order, conventions of grammar/writing sentences
Directions: If necessary, read the directions for each part. When students have completed the page, present each item and the answer. Correct any errors.

Part 3

Draw in the arrows. Shade in each tube that carries dark blood. Tell if each tube is a vein or an artery.

1. _____

2. _____

3. _____

4. _____

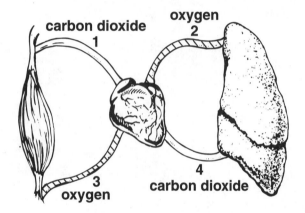

carbon dioxide 1

oxygen 2

3 **oxygen**

4 **carbon dioxide**

Part 4

Circle the subject and underline the predicate in each sentence. Rewrite each sentence by moving the predicate.

1. Tom and Roberto went skating last night.

_____

_____

2. The man and the woman have been running for ten minutes.

_____

_____

3. Doug was happy because he made the team.

_____

_____

Part 5

Write a word that comes from **explain** in each blank. Then fill in the circle beside **verb, noun,** or **adjective.**

1. She is _____ to the doctor what hurts.

   ◯ verb   ◯ noun   ◯ adjective

2. Her _____ was easy to understand.

   ◯ verb   ◯ noun   ◯ adjective

3. Don wrote an _____ letter to the city council.

   ◯ verb   ◯ noun   ◯ adjective

Graphic aids, conventions of grammar/writing sentences, inflectional/derivational suffixes
Directions: If necessary, read the directions for each part. When students have completed the page, present each item and the answer. Correct any errors.

Part 1

Write the middle part of each deduction.

1. Giant apes like to eat bananas.

_____

_____

So, Gog likes to eat bananas.

2. Professional baseball players make a great deal of money.

_____

_____

So, he makes a great deal of money.

3. People who eat oranges get vitamin C.

_____

_____

So, Sheryl gets vitamin C.

Part 2

Tell which fact each statement relates to.

> 1. **Tom wants his quadriceps bigger.**
>
> 2. **Ted was breathing the clean mountain air.**

1. The oxygen went into his lungs. _____

2. He wants to work on a four-headed muscle. _____

3. The muscle covers the back of his femur. _____

Part 3

Underline the common part. Fill in the circle beside the word that combines the sentences correctly. Combine the sentences with that word.

1. Dolphins are not fish.

Dolphins live in the water.

○ **but**   ○ **which**   ○ **because**

_____

_____

2. Matthew is an experienced babysitter.

Matthew has two younger sisters.

○ **because**   ○ **which**   ○ **who**

_____

_____

3. Molly didn't watch the movie.

The movie was very scary.

○ **who**   ○ **because**   ○ **and**

_____

_____

4. Bologna is my favorite sandwich.

Today I am eating a cheese sandwich.

○ **who**   ○ **but**   ○ **which**

_____

_____

Identifying/making assumptions, evaluating statements, conventions of grammar/writing sentences
Directions: If necessary, read the directions for each part. When students have completed the page, present each item and the answer. Correct any errors.

51

Part 4
Fill in each blank.

1. _____
2. _____
3. _____
4. _____
5. _____
6. _____

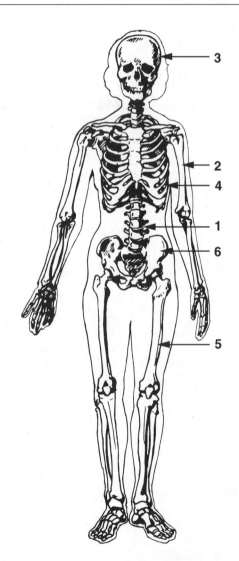

☆ Part 5
Number the words in each group in **alphabetical order**. The first one is done for you.

    3   4   2   1
1. whale, where, weary, water

2. school, sailor, second, safety

3. recess, rose, ring, reminder

4. earth, earn, ease, each

5. mist, mite, mixture, mischief

Part 6
Tell whether each action is controlled by a **sense** nerve or a **motor** nerve. Fill in the correct circle.

1. "Close eyes." ◯ sense ◯ motor
2. "Nod head." ◯ sense ◯ motor
3. "See light." ◯ sense ◯ motor
4. "Wrist hurts." ◯ sense ◯ motor

Graphic aids, alphabetical order, information
Directions: If necessary, read the directions for each part. When students have completed the page, present each item and the answer. Correct any errors.

Part 1

Write the conclusion of each deduction.

1. Things need oxygen in order to burn.

   Candles burn.

   _____

   _____

2. Containers hold things.

   A cup is a container.

   _____

   _____

3. Things made from milk contain vitamin D.

   Cheese is made from milk.

   _____

   _____

Part 2

Make up a simile for each item.

1. Her hair is soft and shiny.

   _____

   _____

2. His hair is extremely white.

   _____

   _____

3. My hands were cold.

   _____

   _____

Part 3

Write a word that comes from **consume** or **modify** in each blank. Then fill in the circle beside **verb**, **noun**, or **adjective.**

1. I assume that vegetables are _____, because many people eat them.

   ◯ verb   ◯ noun   ◯ adjective

2. Charles _____ his bike so he would have a better chance of winning.

   ◯ verb   ◯ noun   ◯ adjective

3. Car manufacturers are trying to impress

   _____.

   ◯ verb   ◯ noun   ◯ adjective

Part 4

Circle the subject and underline the predicate in each sentence. Rewrite each sentence by moving the predicate.

1. The price of grapes will rise after the drought.

   _____

   _____

2. Blood that is almost black carries carbon dioxide throughout the body.

   _____

   _____

3. Tabitha's ice-cream shop buys fifty gallons of milk each week.

   _____

   _____

Evaluate statements, figurative language/simile, conventions of grammar/writing sentences
Directions: If necessary, read the directions for each part. When students have completed the page, present each item and the answer. Correct any errors.

Part 5

Write the instructions.

②
consume

①

digest
③

1. (what) _____

_____

2. (what and where) _____

_____

3. (what and where) _____

_____

☆ Part 6

- An **abbreviation** is the shortened form of a word.
- Use a capital letter to begin an abbreviation for a title of respect or an abbreviation for the name of a place. Use a period at the end of these abbreviations.

  Examples: Ms., Mrs., Dr., Short St.

Write the names correctly.

1. e m Thomas _____

2. ms t crotty _____

3. Princeton road _____

Part 7

Underline the common part. Fill in the circle beside the word that combines the sentences correctly. Combine the sentences with that word.

1. The train was moving slowly.

   The car was moving slowly.

   ○ **who**   ○ **and**   ○ **because**

   _____

   _____

2. Carla's story was bad.

   Dan read Carla's story.

   ○ **because**   ○ **which**   ○ **who**

   _____

   _____

3. Many birds don't like cold weather.

   Many birds fly south before winter starts.

   ○ **who**   ○ **because**   ○ **which**

   _____

   _____

4. Shanece is the smartest student in the class.

   Shanece is my best friend.

   ○ **who**   ○ **but**   ○ **which**

   _____

   _____

Writing directions, abbreviations, conventions of grammar/writing sentences
Directions: If necessary, read the directions for each part. When students have completed the page, present each item and the answer. Correct any errors.

Part 1

Read the story and answer the questions.
Write **W** after each question that is answered by words in the story, and underline those words.
Write **D** after each question that is answered by a deduction.

> **Before Bill made a kite, he got a book on kite building and studied it for a long time. The first kite Bill constructed was a Chinese snake kite. It had a tail that was ten meters long. The tail got tangled up in a tree, and Bill lost the kite. So he made a box kite. It was the highest-flying kite he made. It went up over two thousand meters. Sadly, the string broke and Bill never found the kite. The last kite Bill made was a diving kite. He could make it dive by letting go of the string. To pull the kite out of a dive, Bill pulled hard on the string.**

1. What kind of kite was Bill's second kite?

_____

2. How many kites did Bill build? _____

_____

3. Why couldn't Bill get his kite out of the tree?

_____

Part 2

Fill in each blank with the word that has the same meaning as the word under the blank.

1. Before the game started, Shawn needed to

_____ a baseball bat.
   (get)

2. Terrance _____ the whole pizza.
         (ate)

3. The factory _____ cars and boats.
       (makes)

Part 3

Write **R** for each fact that is **relevant** to what happened. Write **I** for each fact that is **irrelevant** to what happened.

> **Sara made a big salad and ate it outside in the warm sun.**

1. Sara lives in Oregon. _____

2. Many of Sara's friends like sports. _____

3. She was very hungry. _____

4. Sara loves to eat lettuce. _____

5. Sara was with her dog Sparky. _____

6. Sara's brother is named Martin. _____

Deductions, context clues, distinguishing between relevant and irrelevant details
Directions: If necessary, read the directions for each part. When students have completed the page, present each item and the answer. Correct any errors.

☆ Part 4

> * Use capital letters to begin **abbreviations** for days of the week. Use periods at the end of the abbreviations.
>
> **Examples: Sun., Mon., Wed., Thurs., Sat.**
>
> * Use capital letters to begin abbreviations for the months of the year.
>
> **Examples: Jan., Feb., Apr., Aug., Nov.**

Write the abbreviations for the days and the months. Use capital letters and periods where they are needed.

1. September _____

2. Thursday _____

3. November _____

4. Monday _____

5. Friday _____

6. October _____

7. January _____

8. December _____

9. Wednesday _____

10. February _____

Part 5

Underline the common part. Fill in the circle beside the word that combines the sentences correctly. Combine the sentences with that word.

1. Cats purr when they are eating.

   Cats purr when they are sleeping.

   ◯ **but**   ◯ **and**   ◯ **because**

   _____

   _____

2. Rick is going to golf with Stone.

   Stone is my brother.

   ◯ **because**   ◯ **which**   ◯ **who**

   _____

   _____

3. Winter is my favorite season.

   I like to ski in the winter.

   ◯ **who**   ◯ **because**   ◯ **but**

   _____

   _____

Abbreviations, conventions of grammar/writing sentences
Directions: If necessary, read the directions for each part. When students have completed the page, present each item and the answer. Correct any errors.

Part 1

For each word on the left write the letter of its definition on the right.

1. arteries   _____   a. (v.) use up or eat

2. capillaries   _____   b. (n.) the tubes that carry blood back to the heart

3. circulatory system _____ c. (v.) guard

4. consume   _____   d. (v.) make something easier to understand

5. digestion   _____   e. (n.) the tubes that carry blood away from the heart

6. explain   _____   f. (n.) the very small tubes that connect arteries and veins

7. heart   _____   g. (n.) the body system that moves blood around the body

8. veins   _____   h. (n.) a statement that tells how things are the same

9. protect   _____   i. (n.) the pump that moves the blood

10. simile   _____   j. (n.) the act of digesting

Part 2

Follow the directions.

1. Draw a horizontal line.

2. Draw a vertical line through the middle of the horizontal line.

3. Draw a second vertical line at the right end of the horizontal line.

4. To the left of the first vertical line, write the verb that means **guard.**

Part 3

Tell whether each action is controlled by a **sense** nerve or a **motor** nerve. Fill in the correct circle.

1. "Slap wall."   ◯ sense   ◯ motor

2. "Watch movie." ◯ sense   ◯ motor

3. "Hair is wet." ◯ sense   ◯ motor

4. "Open mouth."   ◯ sense   ◯ motor

5. "Smell grass." ◯ sense   ◯ motor

Definitions, following directions, information
Directions: If necessary, read the directions for each part. When students have completed the page, present each item and the answer. Correct any errors.

57

☆ Part 4

Rewrite the abbreviations. Use capital letters and periods where needed.

1. aug _____

2. smith rd _____

3. mr c lee _____

4. fri _____

5. dr a roberts _____

6. ms n lincoln _____

7. apr _____

Part 5

Write a word that comes from **manufacture** in each blank. Fill in the circle beside **noun, verb,** or **adjective.**

1. My grandfather _____ candy.

   ◯ noun   ◯ verb   ◯ adjective

2. He has been _____ candy

   for twenty years.

   ◯ noun   ◯ verb   ◯ adjective

3. When I grow up, I want to be a candy

   _____, too.

   ◯ noun   ◯ verb   ◯ adjective

Part 6

Read the story and answer the questions. Write **W** after each question that is answered by words in the story, and underline those words.

Write **D** after each question that is answered by a deduction.

> The pulmonary vein is part of the circulatory system. It carries blood from the lungs to the heart. It is the only vein in the body that carries oxygen. It is also one of the biggest veins in the body.

1. What system does the pulmonary vein

   belong to? _____

   _____

2. What gas do other veins carry? _____

   _____

3. How does blood get from the lungs to the

   heart? _____

   _____

Abbreviations, inflectional and derivational suffixes, deductions
Directions: If necessary, read the directions for each part. When students have completed the page, present each item and the answer. Correct any errors.

58

Part 1

Write a word that comes from **protect** in each blank. Fill in the correct circle beside **noun, verb,** or **adjective**.

1. A body guard is a person who

_____another person.

○ noun   ○ verb   ○ adjective

2. A hat will give _____ from the cold.

○ noun   ○ verb   ○ adjective

3. Catchers wear _____ gear to help them avoid being injured.

○ noun   ○ verb   ○ adjective

Part 2

Tell **two** ways that the things compared are **not** the same.
Tell **one** way that the things compared **are** the same.

| **The wind howled like a wolf.** |

1. _____

_____

2. _____

_____

3. _____

_____

Part 3

Underline the contradiction. Circle the statement it contradicts. Tell **why** the underlined statement contradicts the circled statement.

> Jerome was a paper clip manufacturer. Every day he woke up at 6 A.M. and went straight to his factory. He made sure that the factory workers were doing their jobs. Jerome liked his factory, which is why he went to work at 10 A.M. every day to talk to the employees. His workers were happy because he paid them good salaries.

_____

_____

_____

Part 4

Circle the subject and underline the predicate in each sentence. Rewrite each sentence by moving the predicate.

1. Henry Ford started the Ford Motor Company in 1903.

_____

_____

2. Louis and his sister came home on a cold winter night.

_____

_____

Context clues, comparisons/figurative language, conventions of grammar/writing sentences
Directions: If necessary, read the directions for each part. When students have completed the page, present each item and the answer. Correct any errors.

59

Part 5

Read the story and answer the questions.
Write **W** after each question that is answered by words in the story, and underline those words.
Write **D** after each question that is answered by a deduction.

> **The man came home at 5:30 on a cold winter night. He started a fire in his fireplace. By 6:00 the room was warm, so he took off his coat and hat. Right then he noticed that the room was filled with smoke. He went outside and noticed that no smoke was coming out of the chimney. The man became very angry.**

1. Was the room **hot** or **cold** when the man got home? _____

   _____

2. Was the chimney working properly?

   _____

3. How long did it take the room to heat up?

   _____

4. How did the man feel about the chimney?

   _____

☆ Part 6

> • A **pronoun** is a word that takes the place of a noun.
>
> • Pronouns that take the place of singular nouns are I, me, you, he, him, she, her, and it.
>
>   Example: **Bill** ate slowly. **He** ate slowly.
>
> • Pronouns that take the place of plural nouns are we, us, you, they, and them.
>
>   Example: The ice cream is for **them.**

Choose the correct pronoun in ( ) to take the place of the underlined noun. Then rewrite the sentence.

1. Mrs. Chapman made popcorn for the class. (She, They)

   _____

   _____

2. Students love to eat popcorn. (She, They)

   _____

3. Ron put salt on his popcorn. (He, They)

   _____

   _____

Identifying facts/deductions, pronouns
Directions: If necessary, read the directions for each part. When students have completed the page, present each item and the answer. Correct any errors.

Part 1

Circle the subject and underline the predicate in each sentence. Rewrite each sentence by moving the predicate.

1. Jaime had to get a loan to pay for his new car.

   _____

   _____

2. Fresh fruits and vegetables are expensive compared to canned fruits and vegetables.

   _____

   _____

   _____

3. Your cousin Evan sold his house a week ago.

   _____

   _____

Part 2

Make each statement mean the same thing as the statement in the box.

> **Simone worked hard and had a productive day.**

1. Simone worked hard and finished many things.

2. Simone failed because she worked hard.

3. Simone spent a productive day working hard.

4. Simone was lazy and had a productive day.

Part 3

Follow the directions.

1. Draw a rectangle.

2. Draw an arrow outside the rectangle that points to the top left corner of the rectangle.

3. Draw an arrow outside the rectangle that points to the top right corner of the rectangle.

4. Inside the rectangle, write the noun that means **something that explains**.

Part 4

Write a word that comes from **explain** or **predict** in each blank. Fill in the correct circle beside **noun, verb,** or **adjective.**

1. My mother _____ how to change the oil in the car.

   ◯ noun   ◯ verb   ◯ adjective

2. What is your _____ for who will win the game?

   ◯ noun   ◯ verb   ◯ adjective

3. Could you _____ how to make a cake?

   ◯ noun   ◯ verb   ◯ adjective

Part 5

Underline the contradiction. Circle the statement it contradicts. Tell **why** the underlined statement contradicts the circled statement.

Last summer, everyone in Mudville wanted a pair of sandals. Mrs. Laredo ran the only shoe store in the entire town. Mrs. Laredo bought many pairs of sandals. For each pair of sandals that Mrs. Laredo sold, her store made a profit of ten dollars. As soon as people heard that Mrs. Laredo was selling sandals, they rushed over to the store to buy a pair. By the end of the first day, Mrs. Laredo had sold six pairs of sandals, for a profit of $300. The store ran out of sandals by the end of the week.

_____

_____

Part 6

Make up a simile for each item.

1. The man cried for a long time.

_____

2. Inside the cave, it was very dark.

_____

3. My steak was very tough and hard to eat.

_____

Part 7

Combine the sentences with **particularly**.

1. Mexico has pyramids.

   Mexico has many pyramids near Mexico City.

   _____

   _____

2. My dad likes to watch football.

   My dad likes to watch college football the most.

   _____

   _____

3. Terrance is happy.

   Terrance is happiest when it is hot.

   _____

   _____

☆ Part 8

Underline the pronouns in the following sentences. Circle the noun or nouns that each pronoun replaces.

1. Betsy lost her kitten.

2. Tim placed his book on the table.

3. Marisa saw her bus coming down the street.

4. It was Jerry's book that was on the floor.

5. Jeff's mother told him to come straight home from school.

Identifying contradictions, figurative language/similes, conventions of grammar/writing sentences, pronouns
Directions: If necessary, read the directions for each part. When students have completed the page, present each item and the answer. Correct any errors.

Part 1

Use the facts to fill out the form.

> Facts: Your name is Zeus Jackson. You
> are eighteen years old. You are applying
> to get into State College. Two of your
> relatives graduated from State College.
> Chess is your favorite pastime. You
> are the president of the chess club.
> Your address is 324 Red Oak Avenue,
> San Diego, California.

Instructions:

a. State which club you are president of on line 7.
b. State your age on line 5.
c. On line 1, write what your favorite pastime is.
d. Name the college you would like to attend on line 3.
e. On line 4, write your address.
f. Write your full name, last name first, on line 6.
g. Write the sentence above that gives information you didn't use in filling out the form on line 2.

1. _____
2. _____
   _____
3. _____
4. _____
   _____
5. _____
6. _____
7. _____

Part 2

Write the instructions.

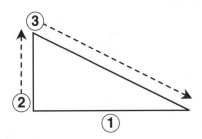

1. (what and where) _____
   _____

2. (what and where) _____
   _____
   _____

3. (what and where) _____
   _____

Part 3

Write a word that comes from **criticize** in each blank. Fill in the correct circle beside **noun, verb,** or **adjective.**

1. He quit the team because he couldn't stand
   the coach's _____ .
   ◯ noun   ◯ verb   ◯ adjective

2. Must you _____ everything I do?
   ◯ noun   ◯ verb   ◯ adjective

3. The art critic _____ Sheri's new painting.
   ◯ noun   ◯ verb   ◯ adjective

Identifying facts, writing instructions, context clues
Directions: If necessary, read the directions for each part. When students have completed the page, present each item and the answer. Correct any errors.

☆ Part 4

Use the pronouns in the box below to complete each sentence.

We	they	Our
them	My	your

1. Did _____ sister get married last summer?

2. _____ elbow hurt all day at school.

3. Where did _____ say the coats were?

4. _____ favorite cousin is coming for a visit this weekend.

5. I saw _____ on my way to baseball practice.

6. _____ went to the museum and the park.

Part 5

Rewrite the paragraph in four sentences on the lines below. If two of the sentences tell **why,** combine the sentences with **because.** If the sentences seem contradictory, combine them with **but.**

> Blue River is the longest river in the county. My house is next to Blue River. I like to swim. I like most to swim in Blue River. Blue River is too deep to swim in right now. There was a bad rainstorm last night. My little brother is afraid of the water and has never gone swimming in the river. My little brother is ten years old.

_____

_____

_____

_____

_____

_____

_____

_____

_____

Pronouns, conventions of grammar/writing sentences
Directions: If necessary, read the directions for each part. When students have completed the page, present each item and the answer. Correct any errors.

Part 1

Underline the contradiction. Circle the statement it contradicts. Tell **why** the underlined statement contradicts the circled statement.

> **Larry is a big rabbit with short ears. All of Larry's friends and relatives have big ears. Whenever they see Larry, the other rabbits can't stop from laughing at how funny he looks with a big body and short, little ears. One day, as Larry is hopping through a garden, he hears a cry for help. When he finally finds where the cry is coming from, he sees his friends trapped under a box. Since he is so small, Larry is able to knock the box over and save his friends. Since then, no rabbits laugh at Larry.**

_____

_____

Part 2

Fill in each blank with the word that has the same meaning as the word or words under the blank.

1. Marvin was very sick and was not able to

_____ anything but dry toast.
(change food into fuel for the body)

2. To make things clear, he _____
   again.   (made easier to understand)

3. I wear a heavy jacket to _____
   me from the cold weather.   (guard)

Part 3

Write the instructions.

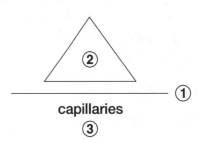

capillaries
③

1. (what) _____

_____

2. (what and where) _____

3. (what and where) _____

_____

Part 4

Make up a simile for each item.

1. She runs really fast.

_____

_____

2. His skin is very pale.

_____

_____

3. The fog is very thick.

_____

_____

4. Her cheeks are very red.

_____

Identifying contradictions, context clues, writing instructions, figurative language/similes
Directions: If necessary, read the directions for each part. When students have completed the page, present each item and the answer. Correct any errors.

Part 5

Underline the common part in each sentence. Fill in the circle beside the word that combines the sentences correctly. Combine the sentences with that word.

1. I am eighteen.

I have the right to vote.

◯ **particularly**   ◯ **which**   ◯ **because**

_____

_____

2. Brazil is in South America.

Portuguese is the official language of Brazil.

◯ **because**   ◯ **which**   ◯ **who**

_____

_____

3. Jamal likes to go skiing.

Jamal likes to go skiing most in Colorado.

◯ **who**   ◯ **particularly**   ◯ **which**

_____

_____

4. Anne is a teacher.

Anne does not like students.

◯ **particularly**   ◯ **but**   ◯ **which**

_____

_____

☆ Part 6

> • A **statement** tells something and ends with a **period**.
>
>   Cody went for a walk.
>
> • A **question** asks something and ends with a **question mark.**
>
>   When will you be done?
>
> • A sentence that shows strong feeling ends with an **exclamation point** and is called an **exclamation.**
>
>   I am so happy for you!

Read each sentence. Write an **S** if it is a statement, a **Q** if it is a question, or an **E** if it is an exclamation.

_____ **1.** What time is dinner?

_____ **2.** We won the game!

_____ **3.** She likes to travel in the summer.

_____ **4.** Did you want to see me?

_____ **5.** I can't wait for the party!

_____ **6.** How do we get to the parade?

_____ **7.** I put my pencils in my desk.

_____ **8.** Watch out for that car!

_____ **9.** It's time to go to bed.

_____ **10.** I want to eat dinner now!

Conventions of grammar/writing sentences, types of sentences
Directions: If necessary, read the directions for each part. When students have competed the page, present each item and the answer. Correct any errors.

Part 1

For each word on the left, write the letter of its definition on the right.

1. manufactured _____

2. lung _____

3. select _____

4. trachea _____

5. bronchial tubes _____

6. conclude _____

7. reside _____

8. examine _____

9. respiratory system _____

10. explain _____

a. *(n.)* the tube that brings outside air to the lungs

b. *(v.)* look at

c. *(a.)* that something has been made in a factory

d. *(v.)* make something easier to understand

e. *(n.)* a large organ that brings air into contact with the blood

f. *(n.)* the body system that brings oxygen to the blood

g. *(n.)* the tubes inside the lungs

h. *(v.)* end or figure out

i. *(v.)* live somewhere

j. *(v.)* choose

Part 2

Follow the directions.

1. Draw a vertical line.

2. Draw a large square on the right side of the vertical line.

3. Draw a second vertical line to the right of the large square.

4. Inside the square, write the verb that means **control**.

Part 3

Write a word that comes from **digest** or **explain** in each blank. Fill in the correct circle for **noun, verb,** or **adjective**.

1. The book includes a few pages of

_____ notes to help the reader understand the text.

◯ noun   ◯ verb   ◯ adjective

2. Do you have an _____ as to why my lamp is broken?

◯ noun   ◯ verb   ◯ adjective

3. This liquid will help your

_____ problems.

◯ noun   ◯ verb   ◯ adjective

Definitions, following directions, context clues
Directions: If necessary, read the directions for each part. When students have completed the page, present each item and the answer. Correct any errors.

Part 4

Read the story and answer the questions.
Write **W** after each question that is answered
by words in the story, and underline those
words.
Write **D** after each question that is answered by
a deduction.

> The Jones Company manufactures
> automobiles. Almost everyone working
> for the Jones Company lives in the town
> of Thomasville. Some workers walk to
> the factory each morning because it is
> only a block or two from where they live.
> The Jones Company produces two
> different vehicles, the Jones Speedster
> and the Jones Minivan. The Jones
> Company makes sturdy cars.

1. What does the Jones Company manufacture?

_____

2. Where is the Jones Company located?

_____

3. Why is the Jones Company's success
   important to Thomasville residents?

_____

_____

4. What two different vehicles does the Jones

Company produce? _____

_____

_____

Part 5

Write the middle part of each deduction.

1. Snow falls when the temperature is low.

_____

_____

So, the temperature in the mountains is low.

2. Citizens who vote are at least 18 years old.

_____

_____

So, Maurice is at least 18 years old.

3. Some birds migrate south in the fall.

_____

_____

So, maybe geese migrate south in the fall.

☆ Part 6

Read each sentence. Decide whether it is a
statement, a **question**, or an **exclamation**. Add
the correct punctuation to each sentence.

1. Which team do you think will win _____

2. What a good player she is _____

3. The ants got the cake _____

4. I'm going to the library after school _____

5. Where did you put my shoes _____

6. Let's run downstairs and hide _____

7. Anna went fishing with her dad _____

8. Did you say we should go inside _____

Identifying/evaluating deductions, types of sentences
Directions: If necessary, read the directions for each part. When students have completed the page, present each item
and the answer. Correct any errors.

Part 1

Fill in each blank.

1. _____

2. _____

3. _____

1 and 3. _____ nervous
   system

2. _____ nervous system

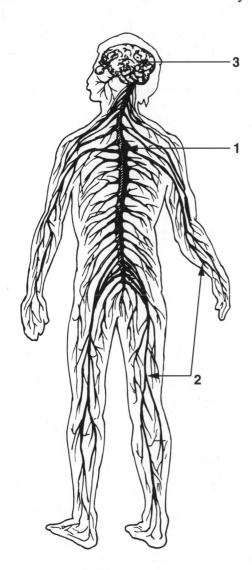

Part 2

Write a word that comes from **participate** in
each blank. Then fill in the circle for **noun,
verb,** or **adjective**.

1. The teacher informed the class that each

   student would have to _____
   in the class play.

   ◯ noun   ◯ verb   ◯ adjective

2. Jim will be _____ in the
   bazaar at his church on Saturday.

   ◯ noun   ◯ verb   ◯ adjective

3. Their _____ was crucial to

   the success of the business.

   ◯ noun   ◯ verb   ◯ adjective

4. She had a _____ role in the
   musical.

   ◯ noun   ◯ verb   ◯ adjective

☆ Part 3

Read the following sentences. Decide whether
each sentence is a question, a statement, or an
exclamation. Fill in the circle next to the
correct answer.

1. This a beautiful picture!

   ◯ statement ◯ question ◯ exclamation

2. My piano teacher said I was doing a good job.

   ◯ statement ◯ question ◯ exclamation

3. How many wishes did you make?

   ◯ statement ◯ question ◯ exclamation

Graphic aids, inflectional and derivational suffixes, types of sentences
Directions: If necessary, read the directions for each part. When students have completed the page, present each item
and the answer. Correct any errors.

Part 4

Fill in the circle beside the word that combines the sentences correctly. Combine the sentences with that word.

1. Kristen was always late for work.

   Kristen lost her job.

   ○ particularly   ○ but   ○ because

   _____

   _____

2. The dog was barking loudly.

   The dog saw a squirrel.

   ○ but   ○ particularly   ○ because

   _____

   _____

3. The coffee shop brews coffee.

   The coffee shop fries doughnuts.

   ○ and   ○ particularly   ○ because

   _____

   _____

4. Scott practices his multiplication facts every night.

   Scott never fails a math test.

   ○ but   ○ because   ○ which

   _____

   _____

   _____

Part 5

Underline the contradiction. Circle the statement it contradicts.

Bright blue liquid flowed through tubes in the lab. Some liquid was hotter than room temperature and some liquid was almost freezing. The lab looked like a jungle. The doctor said, "I know that all this liquid has the same amount of carbon dioxide. The reason is that all the liquid is now 56 degrees. If I get that carbon dioxide out of the liquid, I will sell it and make money."

Conventions of grammar/writing sentences, identifying contradictions
Directions: If necessary, read the directions for each part. When students have completed the page, present each item and the answer. Correct any errors.

Part 1

Tell **one** way that the things compared are **not** the same.
Tell **one** way that the things compared **are** the same.

> **Before the storm, the sky was like a bruise.**

1. _____

   _____

2. _____

   _____

Part 2

Circle the subject and underline the predicate in each sentence. Rewrite each sentence by moving part of the predicate.

1. Her grandma and her aunt are coming to visit in a week.

   _____

   _____

2. My mom always goes jogging after work.

   _____

   _____

3. You should always look both ways before crossing a street.

   _____

   _____

Part 3

For each sentence, write **two** sentences that have the underlined common part.

1. Dan, who is very athletic, runs a marathon every year.

   a. _____

   _____

   b. _____

   _____

2. Tiffany got a raise and a bigger office.

   a. _____

   _____

   b. _____

   _____

3. Rachel, who is in sales, does a great deal of traveling for her job.

   a. _____

   _____

   b. _____

   _____

Figurative language/similes, conventions of grammar, writing sentences
Directions: If necessary, read the directions for each part. When students have completed the page, present each item and the answer. Correct any errors.

☆ Part 4

> An **adjective** is a word that describes a noun. It tells which one, how many, or what kind.
>
> The **blue** car   My **kind** brother
>
> Our **new** house   The **big** park

Read the sentences. Circle the adjective that describes the underlined noun.

1. The gray <u>cat</u> slept in the sun.

2. The tiny <u>baby</u> smiled at me.

3. The big <u>icicle</u> was hanging from the roof.

4. I am carrying four <u>books</u>.

5. The sick <u>boy</u> went home at lunch.

6. Can you find the new <u>flag</u>?

7. The yellow <u>bird</u> ate from the feeder.

8. The apple <u>tree</u> was by the garage.

9. Rose likes to eat warm <u>cookies</u>.

10. Teresa wants to open two <u>presents</u>.

Part 5

Fill in each blank with the word that has the same meaning as the word or words under the blank.

1. They wanted to _____ in a quiet
   (live somewhere)

   neighborhood.

2. Denise wanted to _____ the papers
   (look at)

   more thoroughly before signing them.

3. The students were asked to _____
   (choose)

   a topic that they wanted to research.

4. The _____ of the movie was
   (end)

   not what she expected.

5. When he didn't understand the

   _____, he asked his teacher
   (something that explains)

   to repeat it.

Adjectives, context clues
Directions: If necessary, read the directions for each part. When students have completed the page, present each item and the answer. Correct any errors.

☆ Part 1

Complete each sentence below with the best adjective from the box.

| blue | happy | secret | new | sandy |

1. The _____ boy blew out all his candles.

2. Did the _____ baby smile at you?

3. My sisters and I liked the _____ car.

4. Our _____ clubhouse is hard to find.

5. The _____ beach did not hurt my feet.

Part 2

Make up a simile for each item.

1. The kitten's legs were very skinny.

_____

_____

2. His hands were very soft.

_____

_____

Part 3

Fill in each blank.

1. _____

2. _____

3. _____

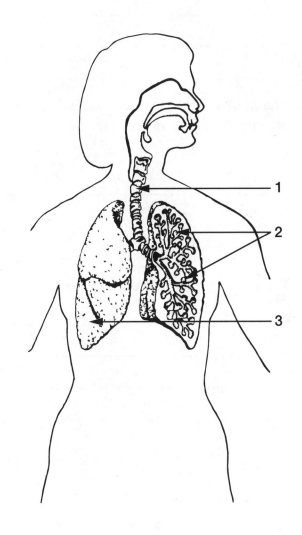

Adjectives, figurative language, graphic aids
Directions: If necessary, read the directions for each part. When students have completed the page, present each item and the answer. Correct any errors.

Part 4

For each sentence, write **two** sentences that have the underlined common part.

1. Heather and Carrie are <u>riding bikes</u>.

   a. _____

   _____

   b. _____

   _____

2. You must follow <u>the directions</u>, which say to do only the odd-numbered questions.

   a. _____

   _____

   b. _____

   _____

3. <u>The movie</u> was scary, but it was very good.

   a. _____

   _____

   b. _____

   _____

Part 5

Circle the subject and underline the predicate in each sentence.

Rewrite each sentence by moving part of the predicate.

1. They built a pool in their backyard.

   _____

   _____

2. Terry and Rich went to a baseball game in New York.

   _____

   _____

3. Driving is not a good idea if you are tired.

   _____

   _____

4. Three thousand people ran in a race last Monday.

   _____

   _____

Writing sentences, conventions of grammar
Directions: If necessary, read the directions for each part. When students have completed the page, present each item and the answer. Correct any errors.

Part 1

Underline the contradiction. Circle the statement it contradicts. Tell **why** the underlined statement contradicts the circled statement. Make the underlined statement true.

Over time, some luxuries become needs. The first people on Earth didn't need much to live; raw meat, water, and a cave. Later, somebody discovered fire, and people started using it. They didn't really need fire, but they liked it. Now they could cook their food and warm their caves at night. Over time they got so used to cooking food and keeping warm that they couldn't live without fire. Fire had started out as a need and become a luxury. The same thing happened with shoes, cups, plates, chairs, beds, and many other things.

_____

_____

Part 2

Write the instructions.

①
_____
trachea   ③
_____
②

1. (what) _____

_____

2. (what and where) _____

_____

3. (what and where) _____

_____

☆ Part 3

Read the sentences. Circle the adjectives used in each sentence.

1. My favorite food is fried chicken.

2. Our old car wouldn't start on such a cold morning.

3. The old dog limped down the long street.

4. The tired hiker tripped on the big rock.

5. A furry rabbit crossed the narrow path.

6. The two skaters glided on the smooth ice.

7. Her long hair was tied in two braids.

8. The little boy ate the last apple.

Identifying contradictions, writing instructions, adjectives
Directions: If necessary, read the directions for each part. When students have completed the page, present each item and the answer. Correct any errors.

Part 4

Tell whether each action is controlled by a **sense** nerve or a **motor** nerve. Fill in the correct circle.

1. "Open the window."   ◯ sense   ◯ motor
2. "Smell cake."   ◯ sense   ◯ motor
3. "Touch the cake."   ◯ sense   ◯ motor
4. "Hear music."   ◯ sense   ◯ motor
5. "Answer the phone."   ◯ sense   ◯ motor
6. "Stomach hurts."   ◯ sense   ◯ motor

Part 5

Fill in the circle beside the word that combines the sentences correctly. Combine the sentences with that word.

1. Today, the sun is shining.

   Today, rain is falling.

   ◯ **but**   ◯ **particularly**   ◯ **who**

   _____

   _____

2. Baseball is considered America's pastime.

   Abner Doubleday invented baseball.

   ◯ **because**   ◯ **but**   ◯ **which**

   _____

   _____

   _____

3. I like candy.

   I like fruit-flavored candy the most.

   ◯ **particularly**   ◯ **which**   ◯ **because**

   _____

4. John was bored.

   John fell asleep while watching the race.

   ◯ **because**   ◯ **which**   ◯ **but**

   _____

5. San Marino is located in Europe.

   San Marino is an extremely small country.

   ◯ **but**   ◯ **particularly**   ◯ **which**

   _____

   _____

   _____

6. Carlos passed the test.

   Carlos won a prize at the science fair.

   ◯ **and**   ◯ **but**   ◯ **which**

   _____

   _____

Information, writing sentences
Directions: If necessary, read the directions for each part. When students have completed the page, present each item and the answer. Correct any errors.

76

Part 1

For each word on the left, write the letter of its definition on the right.

1. consumable _____
2. participation _____
3. supply _____
4. predict _____
5. demand _____
6. obtain _____
7. construct _____
8. manufacture _____

a. *(v.)* say that something will happen

b. *(v.)* build

c. *(n.)* the act of participating

d. *(v.)* make in a factory

e. *(a.)* that something can be consumed

f. *(n.)* how much there is of something

g. *(v.)* get

h. *(n.)* how well something sells

☆ Part 2

> An **adverb** describes a verb. It may answer the question *how, how often, when,* or *where.*

Read the sentences. Circle the adverb or adverbs used in each sentence, and tell whether each adverb answers the question **how, how often, when** or **where.** The first one is done for you.

1. We finally arrived at the hotel.   <u>When</u>

2. He quickly finished his homework.

   _____

3. My cat ran away. _____

4. The band played loudly. _____

5. Don't run near the river. _____

6. I get up early in the morning. _____

Part 3

Write a word that comes from **participate** or **manufacture** in each blank. Fill in the correct circle for **noun, verb,** or **adjective.**

1. Yesterday, I _____ in a soccer match against my cousin's team.

   ◯ **noun**   ◯ **verb**   ◯ **adjective**

2. Tyrone is a _____ of solid wood furniture.

   ◯ **noun**   ◯ **verb**   ◯ **adjective**

3. _____ in the new club has been less than we had hoped.

   ◯ **noun**   ◯ **verb**   ◯ **adjective**

4. Chan _____ in many different clubs at school last year.

   ◯ **noun**   ◯ **verb**   ◯ **adjective**

Definitions, adverbs, conventions of grammar/context clues
Directions: If necessary, read the directions for each part. When students have completed the page, present each item and the answer. Correct any errors.

Part 4

Underline the common part. For each sentence, write **two** sentences with that common part.

1. Manny, who is from Colombia, likes to watch television.

   a. _____

   _____

   b. _____

   _____

2. Sheila joined the choir at her school because she likes to sing.

   a. _____

   _____

   b. _____

   _____

3. The boat crashed into a hidden rock, but it did not sink.

   a. _____

   _____

   b. _____

   _____

Part 5

Use the facts to fill out the form.

> **Facts: You are auditioning for the role of a television superhero. All your life, you have dreamed of being a superhero. You have been acting in plays for ten years. The director of the television show once hired your wife to appear in a commercial. You are twenty-six years old. Your name is Damon Stevens. Your address is 449 Liverpool Avenue, Fremont, California.**

Instructions:
a. Print your address on line 1.
b. Write what you are auditioning for on line 7.
c. On line 3, state what you have always dreamed of being.
d. State your age on line 5.
e. On line 2, tell how many years of acting experience you have.
f. Write your full name on line 4.

1. _____

   _____

2. _____

3. _____

4. _____

5. _____

6. _____

Conventions of grammar/writing sentences, identifying facts
Directions: If necessary, read the directions for each part. When students have completed the page, present each item and the answer. Correct any errors.

Part 1
Underline the redundant sentences.

> After a long day working in his fields, Farmer John is ready to take a nap. When he arrives at his house, he cooks himself some dinner. He is very tired from working so hard in his fields. John has two sisters, Edna and Martha, who like to help him work in his fields and feed his horses. Edna lives in a blue house next to John's farm, and Martha lives in a small house in town. Martha's house is very small. Her favorite part of the day is when she goes out to John's farm to ride her horse, Majestic. Edna enjoys plowing John's cornfields, particularly the field between the river and the forest. Edna likes to look at the river and the trees while she works in the fields.

☆ Part 2
Finish each sentence by choosing an **adverb** from the word box and writing it in the blank.

somewhere Yesterday perfectly carefully

1. _____ Dad and I went grocery shopping.

2. Tom lost his coat _____ near the school.

3. The art teacher _____ cut the tissue paper with her scissors.

4. Margaret skated _____. She made no mistakes.

Part 3
Read the story and answer the questions.
Write **W** after each question that is answered by words in the story, and underline those words.
Write **D** after each question that is answered by a deduction.

> **David tried to be a smart shopper. Good shoppers get more and spend less. Before he went shopping, David read a consumer report about buying food. When he went shopping, David looked for the best deals. He bought grade B eggs because they were cheaper than grade A eggs but just as good. He acquired a big bag of flour because the big bag cost less per pound. David paid a lot of money for the food he bought, but he would have paid a lot more if he hadn't been such a smart shopper.**

1. Was David a smart shopper? _____

_____

2. Why did David buy grade B eggs? _____

_____

3. Green bananas cost $.29 per pound. Ripe bananas cost $.39 per pound. Which kind of

bananas did David buy? _____

_____

Conventions of grammar/revising, adverbs, identifying facts
Directions: If necessary, read the directions for each part. When students have competed the page, present each item and the answer. Correct any errors.

Part 4

Rewrite the paragraph in four sentences on the lines below. If one of the sentences tells **why**, combine the sentences with **because.** If the sentences seem contradictory, combine them with **but.**

Monroe and Sharon like horses. Monroe and Sharon like quarter horses the most. They own eight horses. They do not like all of them. Monroe has been training his horse for months. Monroe will compete in a contest on Saturday. The contest will take place in Columbus. Columbus is the capital of Ohio.

_____

_____

_____

_____

_____

_____

_____

_____

Part 5

1. What's the rule about when the supply is greater than the demand?

_____

_____

_____

In the summer, the supply of snow shovels is greater than the demand for snow shovels.

---

2. What will happen to the price of shovels?

_____

3. How do you know?

_____

_____

Due to last year's flood, the demand for corn is greater than the supply of corn.

---

4. What will happen to the price of corn?

_____

5. How do you know?

_____

_____

Conventions of grammar/writing, drawing conclusions based on evidence
Directions: If necessary, read the directions for each part. When students have completed the page, present each item and the answer. Correct any errors.

Part 1

Write a word that comes from **manufacture** or **participate** in each blank. Fill in the circle for **noun, verb,** or **adjective**.

1. Class _____ is required in order to earn an "A."

   ◯ noun   ◯ verb   ◯ adjective

2. America and Japan _____ thousands of cars each week.

   ◯ noun   ◯ verb   ◯ adjective

3. It is important for airplane

   _____ to follow certain rules and regulations.

   ◯ noun   ◯ verb   ◯ adjective

4. If people work for a bike _____ plant, they make bikes.

   ◯ noun   ◯ verb   ◯ adjective

5. All fourth graders will _____ in the science fair this spring.

   ◯ noun   ◯ verb   ◯ adjective

Part 2

Underline the contradiction. Circle the statement it contradicts. Tell **why** the underlined statement contradicts the circled statement. Make the underlined statement true.

> Corn farmers have to protect their crops from many different bugs. Many times in the past, bugs have wiped out corn crops. Last year, bugs ate a lot of corn, and there was not enough corn for everybody who wanted it. The price of corn was very high. The farmers tried everything to get rid of the bugs. They sprayed powder from planes. They tried to find animals that would eat the bugs. Because there was so little corn, the price of corn continued to drop. One company started manufacturing seeds that were bugproof. All in all, it was a very bad year for farmers.

_____

_____

Part 3

Follow the directions.

1. Draw a rectangle.

2. Draw a vertical line through the middle of the rectangle.

3. Draw a horizontal line through the middle of the vertical line.

4. In the bottom left part of the rectangle, write the word that means **make in a factory**.

Inflectional and derivational suffixes, contradictions, following directions
Directions: If necessary, read the directions for each part. When students have completed the page, present each item and the answer. Correct any errors.

☆ Part 4

Complete each sentence with an **adverb** from the box below. Choose an adverb that answers the question in ( ). Answers may vary.

far	early	quickly
near	late	slowly

1. Jim walked _____. (How?)

2. I got home _____ from cheerleading practice. (When?)

3. The fire was _____ the center of town. (Where?)

4. Sheila ran _____ to her bike. (How?)

5. It was _____ by the time we ate dinner. (When?)

6. We live _____ from the school. (Where?)

Part 5

Tell **two** ways that the things compared **are** the same. Tell **one** way that they are **not** the same.

Her teeth were like snow.

1. _____

2. _____

3. _____

Part 6

Write the conclusion of each deduction.

1. Some doctors perform surgery.

   David is a doctor.

   _____

   _____

2. Vegetables grow in gardens.

   A carrot is a vegetable.

   _____

   _____

3. Mammals are animals that have hair.

   Dogs have hair.

   _____

   _____

Adverbs, figurative language, drawing conclusions
Directions: If necessary, read the directions for each part. When students have completed the page, present each item and the answer. Correct any errors.

82

Part 1

Underline the redundant sentences.

Last summer, everybody in Centerville wanted a pair of sandals. Mr. Jones ran the only shoe store in town. There was a big demand for sandals. Mr. Jones got lots of sandals from a manufacturer. No other place in town sold sandals. Mr. Jones made one dollar on each pair of sandals that he sold. One day, Mr. Jones sold ninety pairs of sandals. He made ninety dollars from sandal sales that day.

☆ Part 2

Facts are details that can be proven true. **Opinions** are what someone thinks. They can't be proven true. Read each sentence below. Write **F** for fact or **O** for opinion.

_____ 1. Whales live in the ocean.

_____ 2. Playing tennis is a fun sport.

_____ 3. Carrots grow in the ground.

_____ 4. Sacramento is the capital of California.

_____ 5. Green beans are good for you.

_____ 6. Fifth grade is the best grade.

Part 3

For each sentence, write **two** sentences with that common part.

1. Jeremy and Carrie have many toys.

   a. _____

   _____

   b. _____

   _____

2. That park, which is on the other side of town, has a lot of trees.

   a. _____

   _____

   b. _____

   _____

3. Patrick fixed his car, which needed new brakes.

   a. _____

   _____

   b. _____

   _____

4. The puppy, which was abandoned by his owner, was hungry and cold.

   a. _____

   _____

   b. _____

   _____

Conventions of grammar/revising, fact and opinion, writing sentences
Directions: If necessary, read the directions for each part. When students have completed the page, present each item and the answer. Correct any errors.

Part 4

Combine the sentences with **although**.

1. Fred was not a fast runner.

Fred won the race.

_____

_____

2. The team lost the championship.

The players were happy the team had a good season.

_____

_____

_____

3. Susan was tired from a busy weekend.

Susan went to the grocery store Sunday night.

_____

_____

_____

Part 5

Follow the directions.

1. Draw a big circle.

2. Draw a horizontal line from the left side of the circle to the right side of the circle.

3. Draw a vertical line from the top of the circle to the bottom of the circle.

4. In the top right part of the circle, write the word that means **use up** or **eat**.

Part 6

Write the middle part of each deduction.

1. Feelings travel on sense nerves.

_____

So, pain travels on sense nerves.

2. Commands travel on motor nerves.

_____

So, "Move arm" travels on motor nerves.

3. Some diseases damage nerves.

_____

So, maybe polio damages nerves.

Writing sentences/conventions of grammar, following directions, deductions
Directions: If necessary, read the directions for each part. When students have completed the page, present each item and the answer. Correct any errors.

Part 1

Fill in each blank with the word that has the same meaning as the word or words under the blank.

1. The _____ of the play
     (end)

surprised the audience.

2. He _____ a video the whole
     (chose)

family could enjoy.

3. Mr. Warga _____ the student
          (found fault with)

for talking in the assembly.

4. Please _____ the solution to
(make things easier to understand)

the math problem to the class.

Part 2

Combine the sentences with **although.**

1. Elizabeth exercised every day.

Elizabeth did not get any thinner.

_____

_____

2. Cody was sick.

Cody could eat his dinner.

_____

_____

3. Terry finished his homework.

Terry did not understand his math.

_____

_____

_____

4. Marcia was sleepy.

Marcia finished the book.

_____

_____

Vocabulary, conventions of grammar/writing sentences
Directions: If necessary, read the directions for each part. When students have completed the page, present each item and the answer. Correct any errors.

85

Part 3

Cross out the wrong word and write the correct word above it. (4)

My dog is a bulldog. Many people is afraid of bulldogs, but my dog is a very nice dog. We goes walking every day in the park. At home, I keep him tied in the backyard, but sometimes he get loose. If you ever see a bulldog with a green collar, that's my dog. Her name is Sam.

☆ Part 4

Read each sentence below. Underline it if it gives a fact. Circle it if it gives an opinion.

1. Pigs do not smell good.

2. There are four seasons in a year.

3. I love homemade soup!

4. There are seven continents.

5. March is the best month of the year.

6. Basketball is the best sport.

7. When hot air rises, it cools off.

8. Thanksgiving is in November.

Part 5

Fill in each blank.

1. _____

2. _____

3. _____

4. _____

5. _____

6. _____

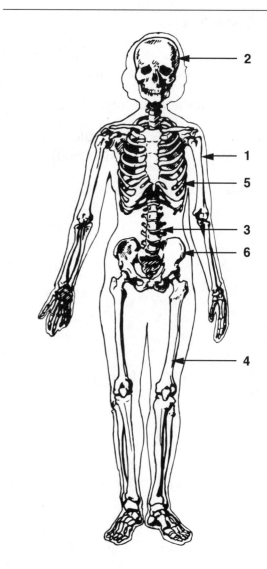

Conventions of grammar, fact and opinion, graphic aids
Directions: If necessary, read the directions for each part. When students have completed the page, present each item and the answer. Correct any errors.

Part 1

Make up a simile for each item.

1. Her eyes are blue.

_____

_____

2. He is so busy.

_____

_____

Part 2

Write the instructions.

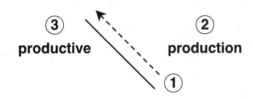

1. _____

_____

2. _____

_____

3. _____

_____

Part 3

Use the facts to fill out the form.

Facts: Your name is Julia Wilson. You have just graduated from State University in Laurelville. Your field is elementary education. You are applying for a teaching job at the local elementary school. You are twenty-two years old. You are newly married and unemployed. Your address is 657 North Broad, Wilmington, North Carolina. You want to teach fourth grade.

Instructions:

1. Name, last name first (please print):

_____

2. Colleges or universities attended:

_____

3. What is your field?

_____

4. Current employer:

_____

5. Address? _____

_____

6. What grade do you prefer to teach?

_____

Figurative language/similes, writing instructions, identifying facts
Directions: If necessary, read the directions for each part. When students have completed the page, present each item and the answer. Correct any errors.

Name _____

Part 4

For each word on the left, write the letter of its definition on the right.

1. participate	_____	a. *(n.)* something that explains
2. circulate	_____	b. *(v.)* breathe
3. respiratory	_____	c. *(n.)* a gas that burning things produce
4. oxygen	_____	d. *(v.)* take part in something
5. carbon dioxide	_____	e. *(v.)* move around
6. redundant	_____	f. *(v.)* find fault with
7. explanation	_____	g. *(n.)* a gas that burning things need
8. respire	_____	h. *(a.)* that something repeats what has already been said
9. criticize	_____	i. *(a.)* that something involves respiration
10. digestive	_____	j. *(a.)* that something involves digestion

☆ Part 5

Read the following paragraph. Draw a line under each sentence that tells a fact. Circle each sentences that give opinions.

Cooking is a lot of fun. Some people are chefs. Their job is to cook. Many chefs go to cooking school. Both men and women can be chefs. Home cooking is better than a chef's cooking. Hotels, restaurants, schools and even airlines have chefs. It would be a fun job to be a chef.

Part 6

Write the middle part of each deduction.

1. Some blood vessels go to the heart.

_____

So, maybe venules go to the heart.

2. Blood that is almost black carries carbon dioxide.

_____

So, blood in the vena cava carries carbon dioxide.

Vocabulary, fact and opinion, deductions
Directions: If necessary, read the directions for each part. When students have completed the page, present each item and the answer. Correct any errors.

Part 1

Underline the common part. For each sentence, write two sentences with that common part.

1. This man and that woman want to reside in town.

a. _____

_____

b. _____

_____

2. He likes his residence because it is old.

a. _____

_____

b. _____

_____

Part 2

meat   leather

1. Tell how the objects could be alike.

_____

_____

2. Write a simile about the objects.

_____

_____

Part 3

1. What is the rule about when the demand is less than the supply?

_____

_____

2. What is the rule about what manufacturers try to do?

_____

_____

3. What is the rule about when the demand is greater than the supply?

_____

_____

Part 4

Circle the subject and underline the predicate in each sentence. Rewrite each sentence by moving part of the predicate.

1. Everyone was cold last winter.

_____

_____

2. Many people walk quickly in New York.

_____

_____

Conventions of grammar, comparisons/figurative language, writing
Directions: Read the directions to each item with the student. Give the student time to respond before going to the next item. When the student has completed the page, go over the items and answers. Correct any errors.

Part 5

Fill in the circle next to the word that combines the sentences correctly. Combine the sentences with that word.

1. Hector acquired a car.

Hector still rides his bike.

◯ which   ◯ because   ◯ but

_____

_____

2. Tom was going to the party.

His friend was going to the party.

◯ who   ◯ particularly   ◯ and

_____

_____

3. That book was predictable.

That book was most predictable near the end.

◯ particularly   ◯ because

◯ however

_____

_____

☆ Part 6

> • A prefix comes before a base word. Here are some examples of words with prefixes.
> **untied   redraw   disobey**
> • The prefixes **un-** and **dis-** mean "not." The prefix **re-** means "again."

Read the word in front of each sentence. Add a prefix to that word and write it in the sentence.

1. heat Should I _____ the soup?

2. fair It is _____ that we can't go to the movie.

3. agree It is all right to _____ when you have a good reason.

4. paint Marcia wants to _____ her house.

5. connect If you _____ the computer, it won't run.

6. sure Susan was _____ of the phone number.

Writing/conventions of grammar, prefixes
Directions: If necessary, read the directions for each part. When students have completed the page, present each item and the answer. Correct any errors.

Part 1

Answer the questions.

1. What's the rule about when the demand is greater than the supply?

_____

_____

> In the fall, the demand for warm coats is greater than the supply of warm coats.

2. What will happen to the price of warm coats?

_____

_____

3. How do you know?

_____

_____

> Last year, the price of gasoline went up.

4. Which was greater, the supply or the demand?

_____

5. How do you know?

_____

_____

Part 2

hair   weeds

1. Tell how the objects could be alike.

_____

_____

2. Write a simile about the objects.

_____

_____

Part 3

Cross out the wrong word and write the correct word above it. (4)

> Last year, Tom had two hamsters. He kept it in a cage. One night, the hamsters got out of the cage. It ran under the bed and wouldn't come out. Tom had to crawl under the bed to grab her hamsters. He pulled them out by their tails and put it back in the cage.

Writing sentences, comparisons/figurative language, conventions of grammar
Directions: If necessary, read the directions for each part. When students have completed the page, present each item and the answer. Correct any errors.

☆ Part 4

Underline each word that begins with a prefix.

1. pack, repack
2. copy, recopy
3. unsure, sure
4. relive, live
5. tie, untie
6. rename, name
7. make, remake
8. untrue, true
9. connect, disconnect
10. disappear, appear

Part 5

Underline the common part. For each sentence, write **two** sentences with that common part.

1. People get cold particularly in the winter.

    a. _____

    _____

    b. _____

    _____

2. Her mother and father are talking about money.

    a. _____

    _____

    b. _____

    _____

3. The doctor checked the man's respiration, which was loud.

    a. _____

    _____

    b. _____

    _____

4. The demand for gas, which is great, increases each year.

    a. _____

    _____

    b. _____

    _____

Prefixes, conventions of grammar/writing sentences
Directions: If necessary, read the directions for each part. When students have completed the page, present each item and the answer. Correct any errors.

Part 1

Rewrite the story in six sentences on the lines below.

German shepherd dogs were first used to protect herds of sheep, which were often attacked by wolves. German shepherds were used by the police, who trained them to sniff out criminals. Today, German shepherds are used as watchdogs and as guide dogs for the blind.

_____

_____

_____

_____

_____

_____

_____

_____

_____

_____

_____

Part 2

hands   ice

1. Tell how the objects could be alike.

_____

_____

2. Write a simile about the objects.

_____

Part 3

Fill in each blank with the word that has the same meaning as the word or words under the blank.

1. Storms _____ the beach.
              (wear down)

2. Did the company ever _____
                          (make in a factory)
   paper?

3. Ted saw the dog _____ his food.
                      (eat)

4. Please do not _____ your sister.
                   (find fault with)

5. Your _____ increases after
          (the act of respiring)
   heavy activity.

Writing, figurative language, vocabulary
Directions: If necessary, read the directions for each part. When students have completed the page, present each item and the answer. Correct any errors.

Part 4
Underline the redundant sentences.

Some people read magazines. Some people don't. The store had many different kinds of magazines. John wanted to acquire a magazine, so he went to the store. The store had a wide selection of magazines. John looked for a magazine about cars. The store had ten different car magazines. John couldn't decide which one to buy. The store had more than one car magazine. John didn't know which one he wanted.

☆ Part 5
Complete each sentence by adding **un-**, **dis-**, or **re-** to the word in parentheses.

1. The man looked _____ about
   (concerned)
   what would happen to him.

2. My teacher asked me to _____ the
   paper.   (do)

3. Terry said that he _____ brussel
   sprouts.   (likes)

Part 6
Follow the directions.

1. Draw a horizontal line.

2. Draw another horizontal line below the first line.

3. Draw a line that slants from the right end of the top line to the left end of the bottom line.

4. On the lower horizontal line, write the word that means **find fault with.**

Conventions of grammar, prefixes, following directions
Directions: If necessary, read the directions for each part. When students have completed the page, present each item and the answer. Correct any errors.

Part 1

Rewrite the story in six sentences on the lines below.

> Diamonds and coal are made of the same mineral, which is carbon. Diamonds are used for jewelry and in industry. Colored diamonds are hard to find because they are quite rare.

_____

_____

_____

_____

_____

_____

_____

_____

_____

_____

Part 2

Write a word that comes from **reside** or **conclude** in each blank. Fill in the circle for **verb, noun,** or **adjective.**

1. The people clapped when Bob

   _____ his speech.

   ◯ verb ◯ noun ◯ adjective

2. Many snakes _____ in warm places.

   ◯ verb ◯ noun ◯ adjective

3. The _____ of the story was sad.

   ◯ verb ◯ noun ◯ adjective

4. Some _____ areas are for older people.

   ◯ verb ◯ noun ◯ adjective

5. Jim _____ that the power was off.

   ◯ verb ◯ noun ◯ adjective

Writing, inflectional and derivational suffixes
Directions: If necessary, read the directions for each part. When students have completed the page, present each item and the answer. Correct any errors.

Part 3

Tell if each nerve is a **sense** nerve or a **motor** nerve. Draw an arrow to show which way each message moves.

1. "Curl toes."   2. "Food smells good."

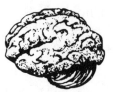

2. "Lie down."   4. "Feel tired."

Part 4

town   beehive

1. Tell how the objects could be alike.

   _____

   _____

2. Write a simile about the objects.

   _____

   _____

☆ Part 5

> • A **suffix** is added at the end of a word and changes the meaning of the word or the way the word is used in a sentence.
>
> thank**ful**   care**less**   teach**er**
>
> The suffix -**ful** means "full of."
> The suffix -**less** means "without."
> The suffix -**er** means "one who does."

Read the base word below. Add the suffix and write the new word.

1. age + less = _____

2. paint + er = _____

3. tire + less = _____

4. joy + ful = _____

5. fear + ful = _____

Graphic aids, figurative language, suffixes
Directions: If necessary, read the directions for each part. When students have completed the page, present each item and answer. Correct any errors.

96

Part 1

Combine the sentences with **although.**

1. Steven interviewed for the job.

Steven didn't get the job.

_____

_____

2. She didn't have all the facts.

Her conclusions were correct.

_____

_____

3. Jessica enjoyed cats more than dogs.

Jessica had a dog for a pet.

_____

_____

4. Carl's sink was broken.

Carl didn't call the plumber for two weeks.

_____

_____

5. It rained the morning of the party.

It turned out to be a beautiful day.

_____

_____

Part 2

Read the story and answer the questions.

> Mr. Jones runs the only dairy farm near Mudville. In January, his cows produce just as much milk as Mudville needs. Mr. Jones makes $1,000 from milk sales that month. In February, his cows produce a lot less milk than Mudville needs. If Mr. Jones sells the milk at the old price, he won't make $1,000 because he doesn't have as much milk to sell. But Mr. Jones wants to make $1,000, so he raises his price. Mudville's demand for milk is much greater than Mr. Jones's supply, and he has no trouble selling his milk at the higher price.

1. What's the rule about demand and supply?

_____

_____

2. If Mr. Jones sells his milk at the old price, why won't he make $1,000?

_____

_____

3. Why did he raise his prices? _____

_____

Conventions of grammar/writing sentences, identifying facts
Directions: If necessary, read the directions for each part. When students have completed the page, present each item and the answer. Correct any errors.

Part 3

For each word on the left, write the letter of its definition on the right.

1. circulate _____   a. (n.) the body system of nerves

2. nervous system _____   b. (n.) something that protects

3. conclude _____   c. (n.) something that is selected

4. protection _____   d. (v.) breathe

5. residence _____   e. (n.) a place where someone resides

6. respire _____   f. (v.) move around

7. selection _____   g. (n.) a statement that tells how things are the same

8. simile _____   h. (v.) end or figure out

Part 4

Write the conclusion of each deduction.

1. Every human heart has four chambers.

   Joe is human.

   _____

   _____

2. Some plants produce resin.

   Trees are plants.

   _____

   _____

3. All nerves carry messages.

   The vagus is a nerve.

   _____

   _____

☆ Part 5

Add one of the **suffixes** from the box below to each underlined word to fit the meaning. Write the new word that is formed.

-ful -ness -er

1. Someone who helps a lot is _____.

2. A person who teaches is a _____.

3. The state of being happy is _____.

4. Someone who paints is a _____.

5. The state of being dark is _____.

6. Someone who likes to play is _____.

Definitions, deductions, suffixes
Directions: If necessary, read the directions for each part. When students have completed the page, present each item and answer. Correct any errors.

Part 1

Fill in the circle beside the word that combines the sentences correctly. Combine the sentences with that word.

1. That con man has sold many phony tickets.

His pal has sold many phony tickets.

◯ however   ◯ and   ◯ which

_____

_____

2. The man took medicine.

The man was sick.

◯ but   ◯ which   ◯ because

_____

_____

3. Minnesota has many lakes.

Minnesota is in the north.

◯ which   ◯ but   ◯ because

_____

_____

Part 2

Underline the contradiction. Circle the statement it contradicts. Tell **why** the underlined statement contradicts the circled statement. Make the underlined statement true.

> When Mel finished high school, he left Columbus for a year. While he was away, construction workers modified every building on Main Street. Many people moved into the city, and the city had to make new regulations. Most people predicted that Columbus would keep growing. When Mel came back, he hardly recognized the city. All kinds of new people were walking on the sidewalks. His friends were saying that Columbus would get bigger. As he walked down Main Street, he noticed that the barber shop was still the same.

_____

_____

_____

_____

Writing sentences/conventions of grammar, contradictions
Directions: If necessary, read the directions for each part. When students have completed the page, present each item and the answer. Correct any errors.

Part 3

Write **P** if the underlined word has a prefix.
Write **S** if it has a suffix. Write **P** and **S** if the
word has both.

1. ____ It is <u>doubtful</u> that anyone will
understand.

2. ____ The <u>painter</u> wanted to move out west.

3. ____ They could not <u>undo</u> what they had
done.

4. ____ The thieves <u>disappeared</u>.

5. ____ She was full of <u>goodness</u>.

6. ____ The teacher said to <u>recopy</u> the letter.

7. ____ The magazine was <u>discontinued</u>.

8. ____ I was <u>fearful</u> of diving off the board.

Part 4

Cross out the wrong word and write the correct
word above it.

Louis Armstrong camed to Chicago in the

1920s. He started her own band. He began to

make recordings. Louis Armstrong's recordings

was probably the most important recordings

ever made. His recordings inspired jazz

musicians all over the country. Soon, many jazz

bands was formed in Chicago and New York.

Part 5

Write the instructions.

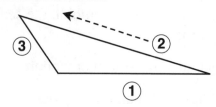

1. _____

_____

_____

2. _____

_____

_____

3. _____

_____

_____

Prefixes/suffixes, conventions of grammar, writing instructions
Directions: If necessary, read the directions for each part. When students have completed the page, present each item
and the answer. Correct any errors.

Part 1

skin   milk

1. Tell how the objects could be alike.

_____

_____

2. Write a simile about the objects.

_____

_____

Part 2

Use the facts to fill out the form.

> **Facts: Your name is Jake Howard. You have lived at 1255 Lake Avenue for two years. Your rent is $400 a month, and your car payments are $250 a month. You were born on October 11, 1973. Your first job, which you started in 1992, was with the American Title Company. Since 1994, you have worked for Juniper Credit, and you make $2,000 a month. You have one credit card, and you are newly married. You are filling out a credit application to buy a washer and dryer.**

Instructions:

1. Name, last name first: _____

2. Age: _____

3. Most recent employer:

_____

4. Monthly income: _____

5. Total monthly rent and car payments:

_____

Part 3

Rewrite the story in four sentences on the lines below. If one of the sentences tells **why,** combine the sentences with **because.** If two sentences seem contradictory, combine them with **but.**

> Finally, Magellan came to an island called Cebu. Cebu is in the southern Philippine Islands. Magellan thought that his trip was almost over. Magellan was still very far from home. Magellan died on Cebu. Magellan got into a fight. His crew fled Cebu. His crew kept on sailing.

_____

_____

_____

_____

_____

_____

_____

_____

_____

_____

Figurative language, identifying facts, writing, conventions of grammar
Directions: If necessary, read the directions for each part. When students have completed the page, present each item and the answer. Correct any errors.

Part 4

Write a word that comes from **predict** or **digest** in each blank. Then fill in the circle for **verb, noun,** or **adjective.**

1. Andy is _____ the winner of the game.

   ◯ verb ◯ noun ◯ adjective

2. Her _____ system includes her esophagus and her liver.

   ◯ verb ◯ noun ◯ adjective

3. She ate peppermint to help her _____.

   ◯ verb ◯ noun ◯ adjective

4. Things that are _____ are often dull.

   ◯ verb ◯ noun ◯ adjective

5. The fortune-teller loved to make

   _____.

   ◯ verb ◯ noun ◯ adjective

6. _____ some food can be hard on your stomach.

   ◯ verb ◯ noun ◯ adjective

☆ Part 5

The first word of a sentence is capitalized.
The wind took my kite into the sky.

The word *I* is always written with a capital letter.

Cory and **I** are going to the play.

Names of people and places begin with a capital letter.
Dr. **M**eek **A**lbany, **N**ew **Y**ork
Franklin **S**treet **C**anada

Days of the week and months of the year are capitalized.
Monday, **M**ay 6; **T**uesday, **W**ednesday

Rewrite the words that should be capitalized.

1. ridge road _____

2. denver, colorado _____

3. dr. ortiz _____

4. north america _____

5. second street _____

6. friday _____

7. mexico _____

8. mr. Carver _____

9. princeton road _____

10. rumson, new jersey _____

Inflectional and derivational suffixes, capitalization
Directions: If necessary, read the directions for each part. When students have completed the page, present each item and the answer. Correct any errors.

Part 1

Answer the questions.

1. What's the rule about products that are readier to use?

   _____

   _____

2. Which is readier to use, a cake or a cake mix?

   _____

3. So, what else do you know about a cake?

   _____

4. How do you know?

   _____

5. Which costs more, a bike that's put together or a bike that comes in parts?

   _____

6. How do you know?

   _____

Mr. Thompson gets cooked pork in a restaurant.
Mr. Rodriguez gets raw pork in a store and then spends an hour cooking it.

7. Whose pork costs more?

   _____

8. How do you know?

   _____

   _____

   _____

Part 2

Underline the nouns. Draw a line **over** the adjectives. Circle the verbs.

1. Burning things need oxygen.

2. That thermostat is regulating the heat in this room.

3. Some burning things produce heat and smoke.

4. The bronchial tubes are inside the lungs.

Part 3

Write a word that comes from **erode** in each blank. Then fill in the circle for **verb, noun,** or **adjective.**

1. The earth loses a lot of productive land

   through _____ .

   ◯ verb   ◯ noun   ◯ adjective

2. We can't afford to let good cropland be

   _____.

   ◯ verb   ◯ noun   ◯ adjective

3. Wind and water are _____ forces.

   ◯ verb   ◯ noun   ◯ adjective

4. Rain can swell rivers and

   _____ their banks.

   ◯ verb   ◯ noun   ◯ adjective

Writing sentences, conventions of grammar, inflectional and derivational suffixes
Directions: If necessary, read the directions for each part. When students have completed the page, present each item and the answer. Correct any errors.

☆ Part 4

Circle the letters that should be capitalized.

1. we all like the story that jennifer told.

2. mrs. hicks is our neighbor and friend.

3. juan and janet are coming over on saturday.

4. the month of november has two holidays.

5. judge king said we had to finish the plan.

6. i wondered whether jessica was going to the opera.

Part 5

fingernails   knives

1. Tell how the objects could be alike.

_____

_____

2. Write a simile about the objects.

_____

_____

hair   cotton candy

3. Tell how the objects could be the same.

_____

_____

4. Write a simile about the objects.

_____

_____

Part 6

Follow the directions.

1. Draw a vertical line.

2. Draw a line that slants up to the right from the bottom of the vertical line.

3. At the top end of the slanted line, draw a vertical line that goes down.

4. To the left of the second vertical line, write the word that means **move around.**

Capitalization, figurative language, following directions
Directions: If necessary, read the directions for each part. When students have completed the page, present each item and the answer. Correct any errors.

☆ Part 1

Circle the letters that should be capital letters.

1. we went to a party for mrs. lee in november.

2. did uncle david come for thanksgiving?

3. they will go to the navesink river in september.

4. mr. casey took his class to riverside park.

5. donna took a boat ride on lake michigan last summer.

6. will grandmother come to see aunt mary?

7. mr. l. h. howard works at knollwood school.

8. the fire was at the corner of second street and main.

Part 2

Write what each analogy tells.

> **What each object is made of**
> **Where you find each object**
> **What makes each object run**
> **What class each object is in**

1. **An engine** is to **gas**

   as **a lightbulb** is to **electricity.**

   _____

   _____

2. **An engine** is to **a car**

   as **a lightbulb** is to **a lamp.**

   _____

   _____

3. **An engine** is to **metal**

   as **a lightbulb** is to **glass.**

   _____

   _____

Capitalization, comparative relationships
Directions: If necessary, read the directions for each part. When students have completed the page, present each item and the answer. Correct any errors.

Part 3

Write **R** for each fact that is **relevant** to what happened. Write **I** for each fact that is **irrelevant** to what happened.

> **Jimmy changed the oil in his car because it cost less than having a mechanic do it.**

1. Jimmy wears gloves. _____

2. Jimmy can change the oil in his car. _____

3. Jimmy has two dogs. _____

4. Jimmy wants to save money. _____

Part 4

Circle the subject and underline the predicate in each sentence. Rewrite each sentence by moving part of the predicate.

1. Ducks, geese, and swans were swimming under the dock.

   _____

   _____

2. The sixth-grade class solved the problem without help.

   _____

   _____

3. Blood turns dark after its oxygen is used.

   _____

   _____

Part 5

Fill in each blank.

1. _____

2. _____

3. _____

4. _____

5. _____

6. _____

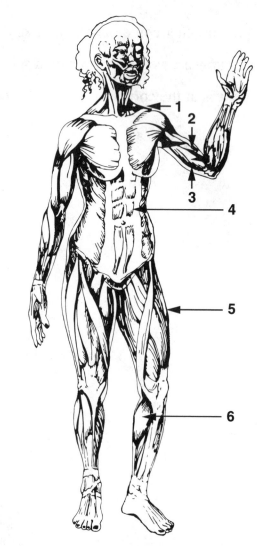

Relevant and irrelevant details, writing sentences/conventions of grammar, graphic aids
Directions: If necessary, read the directions for each part. When students have completed the page, present each item and the answer. Correct any errors.

Part 1

For each word on the left, write the letter of its definition on the right.

1. brain _____
2. constructive _____
3. erode _____
4. examine _____
5. nerve _____
6. predictable _____
7. spinal cord _____
8. consume _____

a. (a.) that something is helpful

b. (n.) a wire in the body that carries messages

c. (a.) that something is easy to predict

d. (v.) look at

e. (n.) the organ that lets you think and feel

f. (n.) the body part that connects the brain to all parts of the body

g. (v.) use up or eat

h. (v.) wear things down

Part 2

Complete the analogies.

1. Tell a part each object has.

   A **car** is to _____

   as a **television** is to _____ .

2. Tell what each object runs on.

   A **car** is to _____

   as a **television** is to _____ .

3. Tell what class each object is in.

   A **car** is to _____

   as a **television** is to _____ .

Part 3

Label each nerve. Write a message for each nerve.

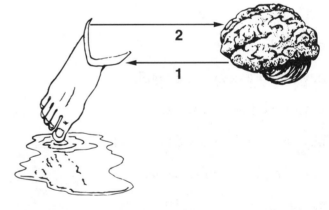

1. _____

2. _____

Definitions, analogies, graphic aids

Directions: If necessary, read the directions for each part. When students have completed the page, present each item and the answer. Correct any errors.

Part 4

Put the statements below the story in the right order.

> Rosa and Sue took their vacation in May. They packed their car with clothes and cameras, and then they started to drive to Mexico. On the way, they stopped off in Arizona. The sun was very hot, so they went swimming. They bought some rugs made by Native Americans. They ate tacos and hot chili. Then they crossed the Mexican border, and they drove toward the sea. When they found a cozy little hotel beside a sandy beach, they stopped. They stayed at the hotel for a week. They ate good Mexican food and swam in the clear, warm water every day.

They ate tacos and chili.   _____

They packed their car.   _____

They found a cozy little hotel.   _____

They drove toward the sea.   _____

They crossed the Mexican border.   _____

They stopped off in Arizona.   _____

Part 5

Write the conclusion to each deduction.

1. Rhonda has had some diseases.

   The mumps is a disease.

   _____

   _____

2. Commands come from the brain.

   "Move leg" is a command.

   _____

   _____

☆ Part 6

> A **homonym** is a word that sounds the same as another word, but has a different meaning and spelling.
> **Examples:** hear/here   their/there

Read each sentence. Then underline the word that completes it.

1. Bill put (some, sum) pictures on the wall.

2. The family has (bin, been) away on a trip.

3. The pitcher (through, threw) his best pitch.

4. My favorite team (won, one) the game.

5. Travis lives in a city (by, buy) the ocean.

6. Erin will (meat, meet) her brother after school.

7. Dan dug a (hole, whole) and planted the tree.

8. Could you (so, sew) this button for me?

9. Tracy's (I, eye) was swollen shut yesterday.

10. Steve grilled some (meat, meet) for our dinner.

Sequential relationships, deductions, homonyms
Directions: If necessary, read the directions for each part. When students have completed the page, present each item and the answer. Correct any errors.

Part 1
Answer the questions.

1. What's the rule about products that are readier to use?

_____

_____

2. Which costs more, a desk that is put together or a desk that comes in parts?

_____

_____

3. How do you know?

_____

_____

Elizabeth and Jessie are both dressing up for a costume party. Jessie made her costume herself. Elizabeth's costume was already made when she bought it.

4. Whose costume costs more?

_____

_____

5. How do you know?

_____

Part 2
Write a word that comes from **acquire** in each blank. Then fill in the circle for **verb, noun,** or **adjective.**

1 Rosa is _____ a lot of money.

◯ verb   ◯ noun   ◯ adjective

2 How did you _____ that rare book?

◯ verb   ◯ noun   ◯ adjective

3 His coat is an expensive _____.

◯ verb   ◯ noun   ◯ adjective

4. Art collectors are _____.

◯ verb   ◯ noun   ◯ adjective

Part 3
Cross out each wrong word and write the correct word above it. (4)

> Many people don't like their jobs, but most firefighters is happy with their work. Most cities has a long list of people waiting to be firefighters. If you are hired as a firefighter, you must spent several months training for the job. You must run, exercise, and climb ropes and ladders. Firefighters mustn't be very strong because their work is very hard.

Writing sentences, inflectional and derivational suffixes, conventions of grammar
Directions: If necessary, read the directions for each part. When students have completed the page, present each item and the answer. Correct any errors.

Part 4

Put the statements below the story in the right order.

> Mike had three rabbits. He kept them in a cage. One night, the rabbits got out of the cage. They hopped under the house and wouldn't come out. Mike had to crawl under the house to grab his rabbits. He pulled them out by the ears and put them back in the cage.

The rabbits got out of the cage.   _____

Mike pulled the rabbits out by their ears. _____

Mike put the rabbits back in the cage.   _____

The rabbits hopped under the house.   _____

Mike crawled under the house.   _____

Part 5

Shade in each tube that carries dark blood. Tell what gas each tube carries.

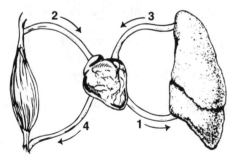

1. _____

2. _____

3. _____

4. _____

☆ Part 6

Here are some **homonyms** you know.		
by	buy	A tree is by the house. Did Bob buy a new book?
hole	whole	The rabbit dug a hole. Tim ate the whole pie.
meet	meat	Meet me at six o'clock. Did dad grill the meat?
one	won	Taylor had one ticket. My cat won a red ribbon.

Read each sentence. Fill in the circle for the word that completes it.

1. My team _____ the championship.

   ◯ one   ◯ won

2. Sally will _____ us in front of the store.

   ◯ meet   ◯ meat

3. We ate the _____ loaf of bread.

   ◯ hole   ◯ whole

4. Dad took me to _____ a new bike.

   ◯ buy   ◯ by

Sequential relationships, graphic aids, homonyms
Directions: If necessary, read the directions for each part. When students have completed the page, present each item and answer. Correct any errors.

Part 1

Circle the subject and underline the predicate in each sentence. Rewrite each sentence by moving part of the predicate.

1. Hank's mother and father played tennis while the sun was out.

   _____

   _____

2. The weather was very dry last winter.

   _____

   _____

3. Many people ride bikes in China.

   _____

   _____

4. You must have a license to drive a car.

   _____

   _____

Part 2

Write **S** before each pair of **synonyms.** Write **A** before each pair of **antonyms.** Write **H** before each pair of **homonyms.**

1. _____   more, less

2. _____   heel, heal

3. _____   false, untrue

4. _____   sew, so

5. _____   late, tardy

6. _____   wait, weight

7. _____   save, spend

8. _____   neat, tidy

9. _____   laugh, cry

10. _____   cent, scent

Part 3

Make up a simile for each item.

1. Her eyes were very green.

   _____

   _____

2. His legs were very long.

   _____

   _____

Conventions of grammar/writing sentences, synonyms, antonyms, homonyms, figurative language
Directions: If necessary, read the directions for each part. When the students have completed the page, present each item and the answer. Correct any errors.

Part 4

Rewrite the paragraph in four sentences on the lines below.

> Last Monday, three men were running a race. They all had sneakers on. The man in the lead was wearing red shorts. The man in the lead had red hair. He said to himself, "If I win this race, I will get lots of money." So he ran faster. He won the race.

_____

_____

_____

_____

_____

_____

_____

Part 5

Write the instructions.

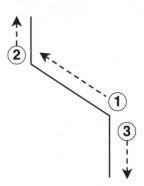

1. _____

   _____

2. _____

   _____

3. _____

   _____

Conventions of grammar, writing, writing instructions
Directions: If necessary, read the directions for each part. When students have completed the page, present each item and the answer. Correct any errors.

☆ Part 1

> Some nouns are **irregular plurals.** Sometimes the spelling changes when a noun becomes a plural. Sometimes the spelling stays the same when the noun becomes the plural.
>
> | Singular | Plural |
> |----------|--------|
> | child | children |
> | sheep | sheep |

Fill in the circle next to the correct plural form for each noun given below.

1. deer   ◯ deers   ◯ deer
2. woman   ◯ womans   ◯ women
3. mouse   ◯ mice   ◯ mouses
4. cloth   ◯ cloth   ◯ cloths
5. goose   ◯ gooses   ◯ geese
6. shelf   ◯ shelves   ◯ shelfs
7. penny   ◯ pennys   ◯ pennies
8. tooth   ◯ teeth   ◯ tooths
9. person   ◯ people   ◯ persons
10. ox   ◯ oxes   ◯ oxen

Part 2

Write the middle part of each deduction.

1. Some rock is made of sand.

_____

So, maybe marble is made of sand.

2. Plants use carbon dioxide.

_____

So, poison oak uses carbon dioxide.

Part 3

Put the statements below the story in the right order.

> Marta was studying to be a doctor. In her first year of medical school, she studied the skeletal system. At the end of the year, Marta was tested on what she had learned. Marta named every bone except the upper leg bone, which she couldn't remember. She passed the test anyway, and she began studying the muscular system. In a few months, Marta could name every muscle and which bones each muscle was attached to.

_____ Marta started studying the muscular system.

_____ Marta could name every part of the muscular system.

_____ Marta couldn't remember what the femur was called.

_____ Marta started studying the skeletal system.

Irregular plurals, deductions, sequential relationships
Directions: If necessary, read the directions for each part. When students have completed the page, present each item and the answer. Correct any errors.

Part 4

Write a word that comes from **reside** or **acquire** in each blank. Then fill in the circle for **verb, noun,** or **adjective.**

1. She needs to _____ a winter coat.

   ◯ verb   ◯ noun   ◯ adjective

2. Many people prefer to live in

   _____ areas.

   ◯ verb   ◯ noun   ◯ adjective

3. The _____ of diamonds is a costly hobby.

   ◯ verb   ◯ noun   ◯ adjective

4. Jane wants to _____ in an apartment.

   ◯ verb   ◯ noun   ◯ adjective

Part 5

Underline the redundant sentences.

The salesman went from house to house, trying to get people to buy brushes. He was not selling many brushes. The man was a salesman. He had a standard sales pitch. He told people that their lives would change if they bought his brushes. Not many people fell for this pitch. The man modified his sales pitch. When he tried to sell his brushes, he gave people a different pitch.

Part 6

Fill in each blank.

1. _____

2. _____

3. _____

4. _____

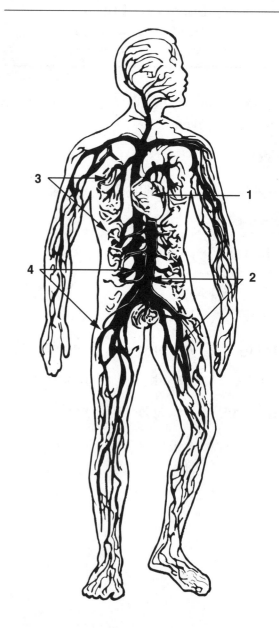

Inflectional and derivational suffixes/conventions of grammar, writing/revising, graphic aids
Directions: If necessary, read the directions for each part. When students have completed the page, present each item and the answer. Correct any errors.

Part 1

Answer the questions.

1. What's the rule about when you buy products in large quantities?

_____

_____

_____

A man buys 10 pounds of poultry.
A supermarket buys 10,000 pounds of poultry.

2. Who buys large quantities of poultry?

_____

3. So, who pays less for each pound of poultry?

_____

4. How do you know?

_____

_____

The store pays $60 for each suit that it buys.
Mrs. Lombardo pays $150 for each suit that she buys.

5. Who pays less for each suit?

_____

6. So, who buys suits in large quantities?

_____

Part 2

Write the plural form for each of the following nouns.

1. foot _____

2. ox _____

3. goose _____

4. tooth _____

5. man _____

Write the singular form for each of the following plural nouns.

6. women _____

7. children _____

8. mice _____

9. oxen _____

10. sheep _____

Writing sentences, irregular plurals
Directions: If necessary, read the directions for each part. When students have completed each page, present each item and the answer. Correct any errors.

Part 3

Use the facts to fill out the form.

> **Facts: Your name is Catherine Bluefield. You are applying for a loan. You rent a house at 1255 Ackerman Road, Phoenix, Arizona, for $500 a month. You work as a legal secretary for a law firm in Phoenix called Brown and Wilson, where you make $1,300 a month. You pay about $100 a month for utilities, $250 a month for a car payment, and $50 a month for washer and dryer payments.**

Instructions:

1. Name: _____

2. Address: _____

   _____

3. Check one: own house ◯   rent house ◯

4. Employer: _____

5. Position: _____

6. Salary: _____

7. Total monthly payments including rent:

   _____

8. Subtract line 7 from line 6: _____

Part 4

Underline the nouns. Draw a line over the adjectives. Circle the verbs.

1. Rosa and Sue took their vacation in May.

2. David tried a new plan.

3. Most people like sports.

4. The doctor examined Berta's leg.

5. Your body uses food and oxygen.

Part 5

Underline the redundant sentences. Cross out and correct the wording errors.

> The zoo owned a giant ape named Gog. Gog was so big that he could jump over houses and lift cars with one hand. One day, Gog broke out if his cage and started walking around the town, crushing mailboxes and fire hydrants with his feet. Gog belonged to the zoo. He saw men loading bananas onto a truck and he roared with joy. The men ran away. Gog wasn't very small, and he could lift men with a single hand. He grabbed six hundred bananas and took them back to his cage. He cage was broken.

Following instructions, conventions of grammar, writing/revising
Directions: If necessary, read the directions for each part. When students have completed each page, present each item and the answer. Correct any errors.

Part 1

For each word on the left, write the letter of its definition on the right.

1. acquire   _____ a. (v.) wear things down

2. production   _____ b. (n.) the end, or something that is concluded

3. criticism   _____ c. (n.) a nerve that lets you move

4. demand   _____ d. (n.) how well something sells

5. explanatory   _____ e. (v.) change food into fuel for the body

6. erode   _____ f. (v.) get

7. motor nerve   _____ g. (n.) a nerve that lets you feel

8. digest   _____ h. (a.) that something has been made in a factory

9. sense nerve   _____ i. (n.) how much there is of something

10. supply   _____ j (n.) a statement that criticizes

11. conclusion   _____ k. (a.) that something explains

12. manufactured   _____ l. (n.) something that is produced

Part 2

Circle each bone that will move. Then draw an
arrow that shows which way it will move.

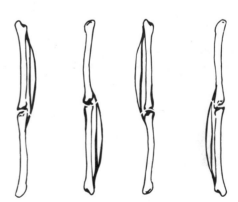

Definitions, graphic aids
Directions: If necessary, read the directions for each part. When students have completed the page, present each item
and the answer. Correct any errors.

Part 3

Underline the contradiction. Circle the statement it contradicts. Tell **why** the underlined statement contradicts the circled statement. Change the underlined statement to make it true.

> The Popper Company was a large toaster manufacturer. Most of the people in Popsville worked for the Popper Company. Joyce worked for the advertising department, and she liked her job. Every day, she participated in basketball games at the factory. Besides taking part in basketball games, Joyce predicted what kind of toasters people wanted. The Popper Company always tried to make people want fewer toasters than it could make. Joyce was very good at writing ads for the toasters.

_____

_____

_____

Part 4

Read each sentence. Underline the correct form of the plural noun.

1. Are your (feet, foots) cold?

2. All the (men, mans) rode on the bus.

3. Three (womans, women) went to the picnic.

4. Terry lost two (tooths, teeth) today.

5. The three (mice, mouses) ran under the porch.

Part 5

Answer the questions.

1. What's the rule about when you buy products in large quantities?

_____

_____

_____

   A supermarket buys larger quantities of meat than a person does.

2. Who pays less for meat?

_____

3. How do you know?

_____

_____

Contradictions, irregular plurals, writing
Directions: If necessary, read the directions for each part. When students have completed the page, present each item and the answer. Correct any errors.

Part 1

Answer the questions.

1. What's the rule about buying products in large quantities?

_____

_____

_____

2. What's the rule about products that are readier to use?

_____

_____

Renee's Restaurant pays $6 per case of catsup.
Shopsmart pays $4 per case of catsup.

3. Who buys larger quantities of catsup?

_____

4. Who pays less for each case of catsup?

_____

Frank's french fries are ready to eat right away.
Frozen french fries take five minutes to fry.

5. Which french fries are readier to use?

_____

6. Which french fries cost more?

_____

Part 2

Fill in the circle for the word that combines the sentences correctly. Combine the sentences with that word.

1. The cat is hungry.

   The cat won't eat.

   ◯ who   ◯ however   ◯ particularly

   _____

   _____

2. The woman is swimming across the lake.

   Her son is swimming across the lake.

   ◯ although   ◯ and   ◯ because

   _____

   _____

3. The femurs support the pelvis.

   The femurs are the longest bones in the body.

   ◯ who   ◯ which   ◯ because

   _____

   _____

4. Wind was eroding the mountain.

   Rain was eroding the mountain.

   ◯ which   ◯ however   ◯ and

   _____

   _____

Deductions, writing sentences
Directions: If necessary, read the directions for each part. When students have completed the page, present each item and the answer. Correct any errors.

Part 3

Tell which fact each statement relates to. Make each contradiction true.

1. Canned corn is readier to use than raw corn.
2. When you buy corn in large quantities, you pay less for each unit.

a. He bought cases of corn to save money. ____

b. He bought a can of corn to save time. ____

c. He bought raw corn to save time. ____

Part 4

Complete the analogies.

1. Tell what part of speech each word is.

   Participatory is to _____

   as **circulation** is to _____.

2. Tell what verb each word comes from.

   Participatory is to _____

   as **circulation** is to _____.

3. Tell what each word means.

   Participatory is to _____

   _____

   as **circulation** is to _____

   _____ .

☆ Part 5

Many words have more than one definition. For example, the word *bark* can mean "tree covering" or it can mean "the sound a dog makes."

To figure out the meaning of the word as it is used in the sentence:

• Look at the rest of the sentence.
• Decide which meaning of the word makes the most sense in the sentence.

Look at the underlined word in each sentence. Fill in the circle next to the meaning of the word that fits the sentence best.

1. Our dog needed a <u>pen</u>.

   ◯ fenced-in place   ◯ writing tool

2. Sometimes the children argued over the <u>ball</u>.

   ◯ round toy that bounces   ◯ a formal dance

3. On her birthday, Julie wanted a new <u>band</u> for her hair.

   ◯ musicians   ◯ thin strip of ribbon

4. Carl placed the coins in the <u>palm</u> of my hand.

   ◯ kind of tree   ◯ part of the hand

5. Emily looks a lot <u>like</u> her sister Laura.

   ◯ to be agreeable to

   ◯ the same or nearly the same

Contradictions, analogies, multiple meanings
Directions: If necessary, read the directions for each part. When students have completed the page, present each item and the answer. Correct any errors.

Part 1

Write **R** for each fact that is **relevant** to what happened. Write **I** for each fact that is **irrelevant** to what happened.

Janice went to Europe on vacation for three weeks.

1. Janice loves to travel.   _____

2. Janice likes dogs.   _____

3. Janice loves to visit new places. _____

4. Janice likes to cook.   _____

5. Janice has two dogs and a cat.   _____

6. Janice did not have to work at her job for three weeks.   _____

7. Janice likes to dance.   _____

8. Janice visited six countries in Europe. _____

Part 2

Write the conclusion of each deduction.

1. Things need oxygen in order to burn.

   A lighted candle is a burning thing.

   _____

   _____

2. Things that burn produce carbon dioxide.

   A campfire is a thing that burns.

   _____

   _____

☆ Part 3

Read the meanings in the box. Write the number of the meaning for each underlined word in the space provided.

---

light 1. Not heavy **2.** Something by which we see
pound 1. A weight equal to 16 ounces **2.** To hit over and over

---

1. _____ He picked up a light piece of wood.

2. _____ It weighed less than a pound.

3. _____ Tim turned on the light so he could see.

4. _____ She used a special tool to pound a design into the wood.

Relevant and irrelevant details, deductions, multiple meaning words
Directions: If necessary, read the directions for each part. When students have completed the page, present each item and the answer. Correct any errors.

Part 4

Answer the questions.

1. What's the rule about products that are readier to use?

_____

_____

2. What's the rule about buying products in large quantities?

_____

_____

_____

The Sporting Goods store buys larger quantities of basketball shoes than the Super-Mart store.

3. Which store pays less for basketball shoes?

_____

4. Which store probably sells basketball shoes at a lower price?

_____

The Sporting Goods store pays $65 for each pair of basketball shoes. The Sports Spot pays $50 for each pair of basketball shoes.

5. Which store pays less for each pair of

basketball shoes? _____

6. Which store buys basketball shoes in larger

quantities? _____

7. How do you know? _____

_____

Part 5

Fill in the circle for the word that combines the sentences correctly. Combine the sentences with that word.

1. The heart works all the time.
The lungs work all the time.

  ◯ **especially**   ◯ **and**   ◯ **although**

_____

_____

2. Her heart beats fast.
Her heart beats fastest when she runs.

  ◯ **particularly**   ◯ **although**   ◯ **and**

_____

_____

3. The regulation protects consumers.
Consumers still get cheated.

  ◯ **which**   ◯ **but**   ◯ **particularly**

_____

_____

4. Robin resides in a fancy home.
Robin acquires many expensive things.

  ◯ **who**   ◯ **but**   ◯ **although**

_____

_____

Deductions, conventions of grammar
Directions: If necessary, read the directions for each part. When students have completed the page, present each item and the answer. Correct any errors.

☆ Part 1

Read the different meanings for each word. Write the meaning of the word as it is used in the sentence.

1. lean: to stand at a slant; to press against; thin

The runner was lean from so much exercise.

Meaning of **lean**: _____

Ted felt somebody lean on his shoulder.

Meaning of **lean**: _____

2. head: the top part of a person's body; to be in front; a person in charge

John's dad is the head of the company.

Meaning of **head**: _____

Betsy bumped her head on a branch.

Meaning of **head**: _____

_____

3. trip: a journey; to stumble and fall; to take quick steps

Jan and Tom took a trip to Ireland.

Meaning of **trip**: _____

A crack in the sidewalk made Gina trip.

Meaning of **trip**: _____

Part 2

Underline the nouns. Draw a line **over** the adjectives. Circle the verbs.

1. The factory is hiring fifteen new employees.

2. My sister ate many carrots and tomatoes for dinner.

3. Many birds fly to Florida every winter.

4. Her father explained his criticism of the new regulations.

5. Her boss runs six miles every day.

Part 3

Make each statement mean the same thing as the statement in the box.

> **Although every person produces carbon dioxide, there is not much in the air.**

1. All people produce carbon dioxide, but there is not much in the air.

2. Although people use up carbon dioxide, there isn't a lot in the air.

3. Every person makes carbon dioxide, but there's a lot in the air.

4. Every person consumes carbon dioxide; however, there is not much in the air.

Multiple meaning words, conventions of grammar, forming generalizations
Directions: If necessary, read the directions for each part. When students have completed the page, present each item and the answer. Correct any errors.

Part 4

Rewrite the story in six sentences on the lines below.

> One day, Ellen fell down the stairs and hurt one of the nerves in her spinal cord. She broke three ribs, and the doctor said that Ellen would have to stay in bed for a long time. He told her that she had hurt a nerve in her central nervous system and he said that she had broken a part of her skeletal system.

_____

_____

_____

_____

_____

_____

_____

_____

_____

_____

Part 5

Write the instructions.

①

③ _____

② **unfortunate**

1. _____

   _____

2. _____

   _____

3. _____

   _____

Part 6

Fill in each blank with the word that has the same meaning as the word or words under the blank.

1. Sarah felt _____ when she lost the
   (not lucky)
   card game.

2. Not wearing a bicycle helmet is

   _____.
   (not smart)

3. I _____ my bike last summer.
   (changed)

4. I failed the test because I was

   _____.
   (not prepared)

5. _____ begins after eating.
   (act of digesting)

Writing, writing instructions, vocabulary
Directions: If necessary, read the directions for each part. When students have completed the page, present each item and the answer. Correct any errors.

Part 1

Put the statements below the story in the right order.

> Claire had just finished high school, and she wanted to make a lot of money. Because so many people ride bikes, she decided to start making bicycle seats. She made 1,000 seats, but nobody wanted them. Claire tried to think of ways to sell the seats. She put ads on television that told how comfortable the seats were. Then she offered a free pen with every seat. Pretty soon, she had to lower her prices. She started to think that making seats wasn't such a good idea after all.

She puts ads on television.   _____

Claire finished high school.   _____

She made 1,000 bicycle seats.   _____

She offered a free pen with every seat.   _____

She decided to make bicycle seats.   _____

She lowered her prices.   _____

Part 2

Fill in the circle for the word that combines the sentences correctly. Combine the sentences with that word.

1. Lynn and her sister met for lunch.

   Lynn and her sister met to go shopping.

   ○ because   ○ especially   ○ and

   _____

   _____

2. Mrs. Ferguson is very wealthy.

   Mrs. Ferguson owns the local newspaper.

   ○ however   ○ who   ○ although

   _____

   _____

3. Melissa consumed lots of food.

   She did not feel full.

   ○ although   ○ which   ○ and

   _____

   _____

Sequential relationships, conventions of grammar/writing sentences
Directions: If necessary, read the directions for each part. When students have completed the page, present each item and the answer. Correct any errors.

Part 3

Make up a simile for each item.

1. The school bus was very slow.

_____

_____

2. The woman in the pool swam very gracefully.

_____

_____

3. Her fingernails were long and sharp.

_____

_____

Part 4

Make each statement mean the same thing as the statement in the box.

> **That factory regulates its production daily.**

1. That factory controls its production every day.

2. What that factory makes is criticized daily.

3. That factory controls its selection every day.

4. What that factory makes is regulated daily.

☆ Part 5

> • To make a **singular noun** show ownership, add an **apostrophe** and **s ('s).**
>
> The girl's bike is red.
>
> • To make a plural noun show ownership, add an **apostrophe after** the **s (s').**
>
> The two girls' bicycles were in the yard.
>
> • If a plural noun does not end with s, add an **apostrophe** and **s ('s).**
>
> The women's club meets on Thursday.

Write the possessive form of each noun.

1. cousin _____

2 teacher _____

3. brother _____

4. workers _____

5. kitten _____

6. boys _____

7. school _____

8. planes _____

9. dinosaur _____

10. doctors _____

Figurative language, forming generalizations, possessive nouns
Directions: If necessary, read the directions for each part. When students have completed the page, present each item and answer. Correct any errors.

Part 1

For each word on the left, write the letter of its definition on the right.

1. acquire _____   a. (a.) that something protects

2. circulation _____   b. (a.) smart

3. fortunate _____   c. (a.) not lucky

4. intelligent _____   d. (n.) the act of respiring

5. protective _____   e. (v.) live somewhere

6. redundant _____   f. (v.) get

7. regulate _____   g. (n.) the act of circulating

8. reside _____   h. (a.) not smart

9. unfortunate _____   i. (a.) lucky

10. respiration _____   j. (a.) that someone or something is careful about selecting things

11. unintelligent _____ k. (a.) that something repeats what has already been said

12. selective _____   l. (v.) control

Part 2

Follow the directions.

1. Print the adjective that means **that someone or something is careful about selecting things.**

2. Draw a vertical line to the left of the word.

3. Draw a horizontal line under the word.

4. Under the horizontal line, print the noun that means **the act of circulating.**

Definitions, following directions
Directions: If necessary, read the directions for each part. When students have completed the page, present each item and the answer. Correct any errors.

☆ Part 3

Rewrite each phrase to show ownership. Add an **apostrophe** or an **apostrophe** and **-s** to the underlined words.

1. a clown hat   _____

2. a snowman nose   _____

3. five dogs bones   _____

4. the pilots hats   _____

5. six kites strings   _____

6. the children   _____

   presents   _____

7. the cats toys   _____

8. the neighbors   _____

   lawn   _____

9. the sisters farm   _____

10. the oxen hooves   _____

Part 4

Put the statements below the story in the right order.

> Matthew wanted to throw a surprise party for his mom's fiftieth birthday. First, he decided when to have the party. He picked Friday night. Then, he bought the invitations and sent them in the mail. He bought streamers and balloons to decorate the house. The next day he bought food for the party and the birthday cake. On the night of the party, he had his dad take his mom shopping while the guests secretly arrived. Once everyone was there, it was safe for Matthew's dad to bring his mom home. When she walked into the kitchen and turned on the light, everyone yelled, "Surprise!" Matthew's mother talked and danced all night long.

The guests at the party yelled, "Surprise!" _____

Matthew decided on a date.   _____

Matthew's dad took his mom shopping.   _____

Matthew bought food for the party.   _____

Matthew sent out invitations.   _____

Matthew bought streamers and balloons. _____

Possessive nouns, sequential relationships

Directions: If necessary, read the directions for each part. When students have completed the page, present each item and the answer. Correct any errors.

Part 1

Follow the directions.

1. Draw a horizontal line.

2. From the right end of the horizontal line, draw a long slanted line up to the left.

3. At the top end of the slanted line, draw a vertical line down through the horizontal line.

4. In the triangle, write the noun that means **something you get.**

Part 2

smile   sunshine

1. Tell how the objects could be alike.

_____

_____

2. Write a simile about the objects.

_____

_____

3. Tell how the objects are not alike.

_____

_____

☆ Part 3

Write the possessive noun that goes with each phrase.

1. the petals on the flower

_____

2. the aunt of the girl

_____

3. the mother of the twins

_____

4. the videos of the boy

_____

Write what each possessive noun means.

1. the sheep's wool

_____

2. the book's cover

_____

3. the boy's friends

_____

4. the sun's warmth

_____

Following directions, figurative language/similes, possessive nouns
Directions: If necessary, read the directions for each part. When students have completed the page, present each item and the answer. Correct any errors.

Part 4

Fill in each blank with the word that has the same meaning as the word or words under the blank.

1. It was very _____ that it
      (not lucky)
   stormed the day of the party.

2. Sheila had to _____ the pile of
          (put in order again)
   papers after she dropped them.

3. Janet was _____ when the
          (not prepared)
   unexpected guests showed up for dinner.

4. It is _____ that it can be
       (not believable)
   seventy degrees one day and thirty degrees
   the next day.

5. When her boss offered her more money,

   Debbie _____ leaving
          (thought about again)
   the company.

6. Marni said that she wanted to _____
   the math problems.   (do again)

Part 5

Answer the questions.

1. What's the rule about what manufacturers
   try to do?

   _____

   _____

**The Barbecue Manufacturing Company
makes 1500 grills a week. People buy 800
grills a week.**

2. Which is greater, the supply or the demand?

   _____

3. What will happen to the price of barbecue
   grills?

   _____

4. What will the Barbecue Manufacturing

   Company try to do?_____

   _____

   _____

**Name two ways that the Barbecue
Manufacturing Company can do that.**

5. _____

   _____

6. _____

   _____

Vocabulary, deductions
Directions: If necessary, read the directions for each part. When students have completed the page, present each item
and the answer. Correct any errors.

LESSON 1 — Name _____

Part 1

Underline the common part. Circle each sentence that tells **why.** Combine the sentences with **because.**

1. The telephone did not work.
   The telephone was broken.
   The telephone did not work because it was broken.

2. Sam drank milk.
   Milk is good for him.
   Sam drank milk because it is good for him.

3. She is riding her bike.
   She has no car.
   She is riding her bike because she has no car.

4. Jeff has a cavity.
   Jeff will have to go to the dentist.
   Jeff will have to go to the dentist because he has a cavity.

Part 2

Circle the subject and underline the predicate in each sentence.

1. The leaves are turning red, orange, and yellow.
2. We watched the toddler cross the room.
3. The digestive system changes food to fuel.
4. That book has many chapters.
5. Months have passed since she has been home.
6. Cars, buses, and trains are methods of transportation.

Part 3

The respiratory tubes branch off into smaller and smaller tubes.

artery capillary bronchial

1. Cross out the word that completes the sentence correctly.
2. Circle the nouns in the sentence.
3. Above the first noun, write the name of the body system the sentence discusses.
4. Underline the verb in the sentence.

1

LESSON 1 — Name _____

Part 4

Underline the common part. Fill in the circle beside the word that combines the sentences correctly. Combine the sentences with that word.

1. Dan likes to play soccer.
   Alex likes to play soccer.
   ● and ○ who ○ which
   Dan and Alex like to play soccer.

2. Nancy likes her bedroom.
   Her bedroom is painted pink.
   ○ and ○ who ● which
   Nancy likes her bedroom, which is painted pink.

3. The boat belongs to Bill.
   Bill gave me a ride.
   ○ and ● who ○ which
   That boat belongs to Bill, who gave me a ride.

Part 5

Fill in each blank.

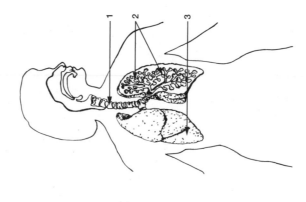

1. trachea
2. bronchial tubes
3. lungs

2

Part 1

Underline the nouns. Draw a line **over** the verbs. Circle the adjectives.

1. The woman (worked) in a small office.

2. A body (has) many organs.

3. People (like) national parks.

4. The respiratory system (brings) oxygen to the blood.

Part 2

Complete the instructions.

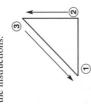

1. Draw a ___horizontal___ ___line___ .

2. Draw a ___vertical___ line ___up___ from the ___right___ end of the ___horizontal___ line.

3. Draw a ___slanted___ line from the ___top___ of the ___vertical___ ___line___ to the ___left___ ___end___ of the ___horizontal___ ___line___ .

Part 3

Circle the subject and underline the predicate of each sentence.

1. (Dogs, cats, and hamsters) can all be pets.

2. (My brother David) plays tennis.

3. (Playing basketball) can be fun.

4. (The trachea and bronchial tubes) are part of the respiratory system.

Part 4

Write a word that comes from **reside** or **produce** in each blank. Then fill in the circle beside **verb, noun,** or **adjective.**

1. Our ___residence___ is a brick house.
   ○ verb   ● noun   ○ adjective

2. The movie ___production___ took ten months.
   ○ verb   ● noun   ○ adjective

3. Did he ___reside___ in that house when he was young?
   ● verb   ○ noun   ○ adjective

4. It was a ___productive___ meeting.
   ○ verb   ○ noun   ● adjective

© 2001 SRA/McGraw-Hill. Permission is granted to reproduce for classroom use.

Conventions of grammar, following directions, inflectional and derivational suffixes
Directions: If necessary, read the directions for each part. When students have completed the page, present each item and the answer. Correct any errors.

3

Part 5

Read the passage and answer the questions.
Circle **W** after each question that is answered by words in the sentences, and underline those words.
Circle **D** after each question that is answered by a deduction.

> **Your respiratory system brings oxygen into contact with your blood. The air goes into your bronchial tubes. Then the air goes into capillaries, which soak up oxygen.**

1. What system brings oxygen to your blood?
   ___Respiratory system___
   (W)   D

2. Where does the air go? Into your bronchial tubes
   (W)   D

3. What do the capillaries do?
   ___Soak up the oxygen___
   (W)   D

4. Is the blood in the capillaries red or dark?
   ___Red___
   W   (D)

Part 6

Underline the common part. Fill in the circle beside the word that combines the sentences correctly. Then combine the sentences with that word.

1. Los Angeles is on the West Coast.
   Oregon is on the West Coast.
   ● and   ○ who   ○ which
   ___Los Angeles and Oregon are on___
   ___the West Coast.___

2. Martha baked cookies.
   The cookies had chocolate chips.
   ○ and   ○ who   ● which
   ___Martha baked cookies, which had___
   ___chocolate chips.___

3. Oxygen is a gas in the air.
   Capillaries soak up oxygen.
   ● and   ○ who   ○ which
   ___Capillaries soak up oxygen, which___
   ___is a gas in the air.___

4. Sam watched his father.
   His father was a baseball player.
   ○ and   ● who   ○ which
   ___Sam watched his father, who was___
   ___a baseball player.___

Deductions, conventions of grammar/writing sentences
Directions: If necessary, read the directions for each part. When students have completed the page, present each item and the answer. Correct any errors.

4   © 2001 SRA/McGraw-Hill. Permission is granted to reproduce for classroom use.

LESSON 3   Name

Part 1

Tell how the things are the same.

1. My hands were like ice.
   They are both cold.

2. His muscles were like rocks.
   They are both hard.

3. The sun looked like a red ball.
   They are both round; they are
   both red.

4. Barb's eyes were like saucers.
   They are both big; they are both
   round.

Part 2

The firefighter put out the fire.

Write **R** for each fact that is **relevant** to what happened. Write **I** for each fact that is **irrelevant** to what happened.

1. The firefighter was old. ____

2. The firefighter used a hose. __R__

3. The fire was in the attic. __R__

4. The firefighter was named Donna. ____

Part 3

Fill in each blank.

1. pelvis
2. spine
3. humerus
4. femur
5. ribs
6. skull

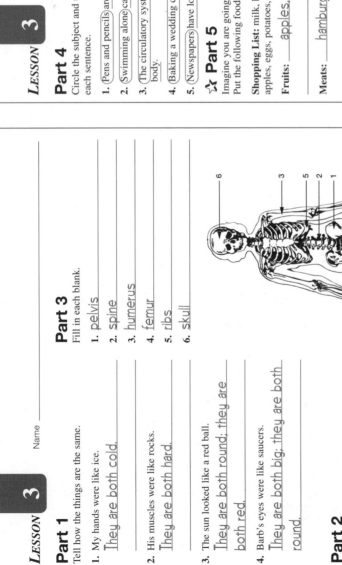

Comparisons/figurative language, main idea/relevant and irrelevant details, graphic aids
Directions: If necessary, read the directions for each part. When students have completed the page, present each item and the answer. Correct any errors.

LESSON 3   Name

Part 4

Circle the subject and underline the predicate in each sentence.

1. (Pens and pencils) are writing tools.
2. (Swimming alone) can be dangerous.
3. (The circulatory system) moves blood in your body.
4. (Baking a wedding cake) takes skill.
5. (Newspapers) have lots of sections.

☆ Part 5

Imagine you are going to the grocery store. Put the following foods in the correct groups.

Shopping List: milk, hamburger, green beans, apples, eggs, potatoes, bacon, bananas

Fruits: apples, bananas

Meats: hamburger, bacon

Vegetables: green beans, potatoes

Dairy: milk, eggs

Part 6

Underline the common part. Combine the sentences with **who**, **which**, or **and.**

1. That mail carrier always walked to work.
   That mail carrier was a young man.
   That mail carrier, who was a young man, always walked to work.

2. Marcia likes to read about horses.
   Marcia rides every day.
   Marcia likes to read about horses and ride every day.

3. The zookeeper liked his job.
   His job was exciting.
   The zookeeper liked his job, which was exciting.

4. David has a new computer.
   David has a new desk.
   David has a new computer and desk.

Conventions of grammar, classifying, conventions of grammar/writing sentences
Directions: If necessary, read the directions for each part. When students have completed the page, present each item and the answer. Correct any errors.

Part 1

For each word on the left, write the letter of its definition on the right.

1. trapezius	d	a.	(n.) the muscle that goes from the ribs to the pelvis
2. biceps	e	b.	(n.) the muscle that covers the front of the femur
3. produce	f	c.	(n.) the muscle that covers the back of the lower leg
4. abdominal muscle	a	d.	(n.) the muscle that covers the back of the neck
5. triceps	j	e.	(n.) the muscle that covers the front of the humerus
6. gastrocnemius	c	f.	(v.) make
7. quadriceps	b	g.	(n.) something that is selected
8. selection	g	h.	(a.) that something regulates
9. criticize	i	i.	(v.) find fault with
10. regulatory	h	j.	(n.) the muscle that covers the back of the humerus

Part 2

Circle the subject and underline the predicate in each sentence.

1. (The pulmonary artery) is a large artery in your body.
2. (Kathy) smiled at her little sister.
3. (To make cider) is hard work.
4. (The heart) pumps the blood.
5. (Dad) walks the dog every morning.
6. (Swimming) is good exercise.

☆ Part 3

Fill in the circle next to the item that does **not** fit in each category.

1. Things to eat with
   ○ plate   ○ fork   ● shoes
2. Things to listen to
   ○ radio   ● pie   ○ television
3. Things to cut with
   ○ scissors   ○ lawnmower   ● comb

Part 4

Tell how the things are the same.

1. Jim eats like a bear.
   They both eat a lot.
2. I slept like a log last night.
   They both don't move.
3. The flowers were like a bone.
   They both are dry.

Part 5

Write a word that comes from **modify** in each blank. Then fill in the circle beside **verb, noun,** or **adjective.**

1. The __modified__ hot rod won the race.
   ○ verb   ○ noun   ● adjective
2. Did you __modify__ the window frame?
   ● verb   ○ noun   ○ adjective
3. They made a lot of __modifications__ to the building.
   ○ verb   ● noun   ○ adjective

Part 6

Fill in each blank.

1. heart
2. veins
3. arteries
4. capillaries

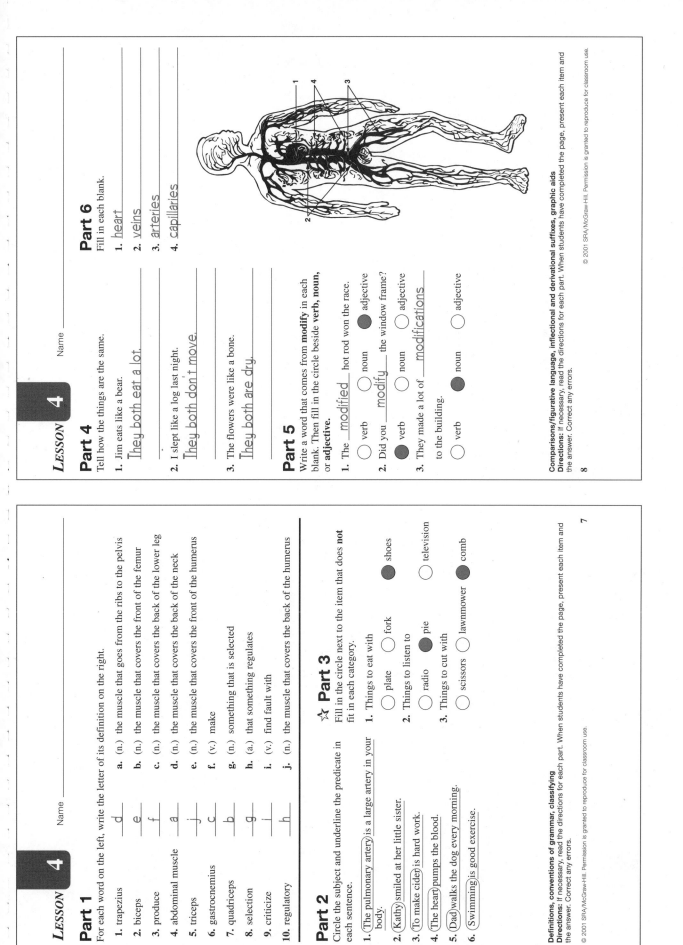

136

Part 1

Underline the common part.
If one of the sentences tells **why**, combine the sentences with **because**.
If neither of the sentences tells why, combine the sentences with **who, which,** or **and.**

1. Jill got good grades.
   Jill worked hard.
   <u>Jill got good grades because</u>
   <u>she worked hard.</u>

2. Brad saw Kim.
   Kim rode her bike fast.
   <u>Brad saw Kim, who rode her bike</u>
   <u>fast.</u>

3. Bob got a new shirt.
   Bob got a new hat.
   <u>Bob got a new shirt and hat.</u>

4. Lane needed a haircut.
   Lane went to the barbershop.
   <u>Lane went to the barbershop</u>
   <u>because he needed a haircut.</u>

5. The race started at ten in the morning.
   I was tired after the race.
   <u>I was tired after the race, which</u>
   <u>started at ten in the morning.</u>

Part 2

Tell how the things are the same.

1. Her smile is like sunshine.
   <u>They both are bright,</u>
   <u>they are both warm.</u>

2. The cake was like a rock.
   <u>They both are hard.</u>

3. John's feet were like blocks of ice.
   <u>They both are cold.</u>

Part 3

Circle the subject and underline the predicate in each sentence.

1. (Babysitting) <u>can be a big responsibility.</u>

2. (To win a game) <u>is exciting.</u>

3. (**Triceps, selections,** and **biceps**) <u>are nouns.</u>

4. (The bike and lawnmower) <u>needed to be</u>
   <u>repaired.</u>

5. (The pulmonary artery) <u>carries carbon dioxide.</u>

Part 4

Write a word that comes from **modify** in each blank. Then fill in the circle beside **verb, noun,** or **adjective.**

1. They drive a <u>modified</u> van.
   ○ verb   ○ noun   ● adjective

2. They <u>modified</u> the van late last year.
   ● verb   ○ noun   ○ adjective

3. We will be <u>modifying</u> our house in the fall.
   ● verb   ○ noun   ○ adjective

4. We plan to make a few <u>modifications</u> to the first floor.
   ○ verb   ● noun   ○ adjective

Part 5

Underline the nouns.
Draw a line **over** the adjectives.
Circle the verbs.

1. <u>Pam</u> (raced) <u>her older brother.</u>

2. <u>They</u> both (wore) new green <u>sneakers.</u>

3. <u>Pam</u> (tripped) on a large <u>rock.</u>

4. <u>Her brother</u> (slipped) on a banana <u>peel.</u>

5. <u>They</u> (started) the <u>race</u> again.

☆ Part 6

Read the list of things. Decide how you could classify or categorize them into smaller, related groups.

football	tennis racket	basketball
wagon	toy cars	dolls

1. What categories could you use?
   <u>Sports equipment and toys</u>

2. What things would you place in each category?
   <u>Sports Equipment: football,</u>
   <u>basketball, tennis racket</u>
   <u>Toys: wagon, toy cars, dolls</u>

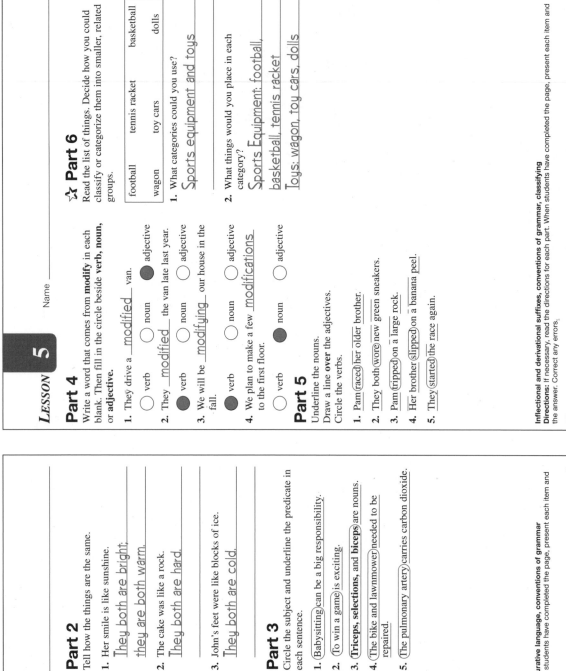

LESSON 6

Name _____

Part 1

Underline the nouns. Draw a line over the adjectives. Circle the verbs.

1. The weather (is) cold and rainy.
2. The car (was moving) in the mud.
3. Two small boys (ran) down the hill.
4. Every student (should have) a pencil.

Part 2

The (pulmonary) **artery carries**
circulatory
dark blood to (the) lungs.
regulates

1. Finish the sentence.
2. Circle the adjectives.
3. Above the second noun write the name of the body system the sentence is talking about.
4. Below the verb, write the verb that means **controls.**

Part 3

Fill in each blank.

1. trachea
2. bronchial tubes
3. lung (lungs)

Conventions of grammar, vocabulary/following directions graphic aids
Directions: If necessary, read the directions for each part. When students have completed the page, present each item and the answer. Correct any errors.

11

LESSON 6

Name _____

☆ Part 4

A compound word is made by joining two words.

Write the compound word made by joining each pair of words.

1. earth + quake = __earthquake__
2. sun + set = __sunset__
3. water + color = __watercolor__
4. star + fish = __starfish__
5. snow + ball = __snowball__
6. egg + shell = __eggshell__
7. watch + dog = __watchdog__
8. air + plane = __airplane__

Part 5

Tell how things are the same.

1. I ate like a pig yesterday.
   __They both eat a lot.__

2. Her voice is like a bell.
   __They both sound clear.__

Part 6

Write **R** for each fact that is relevant to what happened. Write **I** for each fact that is irrelevant to what happened.

Thomas likes pizza and ice cream.

1. Thomas has a younger sister.   I
2. Thomas needs to lose weight.   R
3. Thomas has a part time job.   I
4. His pants don't fit.   R
5. His mom is a good cook.   R

Compound words, comparisons/figurative language, main idea/relevant details.
Directions: If necessary, read the directions for each part. When students have completed the page, present each item and the answer. Correct any errors.

12

LESSON 7

Name _____

Part 1

Tell **two** ways that the things compared are **not** the same. Tell **one** way that the things compared **are the same.**

The cat cried like a baby.

1. A cat is not __a person__ .

2. A baby is not __a pet__ .

3. __Both can cry__ .

Part 2

Write a word that comes from **predict** or **modify** in each blank. Then fill in the circle beside **verb**, **noun**, or **adjective.**

1. He __predicted__ the snowstorm.
   ● verb ○ noun ○ adjective

2. They plan to __modify__ the garage.
   ● verb ○ noun ○ adjective

3. My __prediction__ came true.
   ○ verb ● noun ○ adjective

Comparisons/figurative language, inflectional and derivational suffixes, following directions.
Directions: If necessary, read the directions for each part. When students have completed the page, present each item and the answer. Correct any errors.

© 2001 SRA/McGraw-Hill. Permission is granted to reproduce for classroom use.

13

LESSON 7

Name _____

Part 3

Complete the instructions.

```
        ②                          ③
        |         conclusion
①  digest
        ④
```

1. Draw a __horizontal__ line .

2. Draw a __vertical__ line at the __right__ end of line 1.

3. To the __right__ of the __vertical__ line, write the __noun__ that comes from the verb __conclude__ .

4. Write the word __digest__ under the __horizontal__ line.

Part 4

Read the story and answer the questions. Circle the **W** if the question is answered by words in the story, and underline those words. Circle the **D** if the question is answered by a deduction.

> A construction worker worked from seven in the morning until four in the afternoon. He had an accident at his job and cut his foot. He couldn't see the cut because his foot was bleeding so much. The blood was bright red. Putting a bandage on the cut did not stop the bleeding. He decided he needed to get help fast.

1. What color is the blood in the arteries of your foot? __Red__   W **D**

2. What color is the blood in the veins of your foot? __Almost black__   W **D**

3. Why is the blood in your veins almost black? __Because it is carrying carbon dioxide__   W **D**

4. Was the worker bleeding from a vein or an artery? __Artery__   W **D**

5. Could the accident have occurred at nine in the evening? __No__   W **D**

6. Did the bandage on the cut stop the bleeding? __No__   **W** D

☆ Part 5

Make compound words from the words in the box and write them on the lines below.

thanks	mark	foot	weed
ball	book	giving	sea

1. __thanksgiving__

2. __bookmark__

3. __football__

4. __seaweed__

Deductions, compound words
Directions: If necessary, read the directions for each part. When students have completed the page, present each item and the answer. Correct any errors.

14

© 2001 SRA/McGraw-Hill. Permission is granted to reproduce for classroom use.

Part 1

In each blank, write the word that has the same meaning as the word or words under the blank.

1. The <u>conclusion</u> of the book was a
   (end)

   surprise.

2. Carla's <u>selection</u> was not a good one.
   (choice)

3. The doctor <u>examined</u> her teeth.
   (looked at)

4. A bicycle helmet <u>protects</u> your head.
   (guards)

5. <u>Modifications</u> to your science
   (Changes)

   experiment are needed.

Part 2

Circle the subject and underline the predicate in each sentence.

1. (Nouns) name persons, places, and things.

2. (Every person's nervous system) is made up of nerves.

3. (To scuba dive) takes a lot of instruction.

4. (Baking bread) is time-consuming.

5. (All arteries) carry blood away from the heart.

6. (Lizards and alligators) are reptiles.

Vocabulary, conventions of grammar, writing sentences
Directions: If necessary, read the directions for each part. When students have completed the page, present each item and the answer. Correct any errors.
© 2001 SRA/McGraw-Hill. Permission is granted to reproduce for classroom use.   15

☆ Part 3

Underline the common part. Then combine the sentences with **who** or **which.**

1. Gretchen is a doctor.

   Gretchen speaks French.

   <u>Gretchen, who speaks French, is a doctor.</u>

2. Your heart is in your chest.

   Your heart acts as a pump.

   <u>Your heart, which is in your chest, acts as a pump.</u>

3. Todd has a new brother.

   Todd lives next door.

   <u>Todd, who lives next door, has a new brother.</u>

4. Nerves are everywhere in the body.

   Nerves carry messages.

   <u>Nerves, which carry messages, are everywhere in the body.</u>

Part 4

Draw a line from one word in the first column to one word in the second column to make a compound word. Use each word only once.

1. note   plane
2. news   cake
3. cup   book
4. paint   boat
5. air   bow
6. rain   brush
7. sail   paper

Part 5

Tell **two** ways that the things compared are **not** alike. Tell **one** way that the things compared **are** alike.

> The loaf of bread was like a rock.

1. <u>Rocks can not be eaten.</u>

2. <u>You cannot build a fireplace with a loaf of bread.</u>

3. <u>They both are hard.</u>

Part 6

Read the passage and answer the questions. Circle **W** if the question is answered by words in the story, and underline those words. Circle **D** if the question is answered by a deduction.

> Blood that carries carbon dioxide is almost black. Blood that carries oxygen is red. However, when you cut yourself, the blood is mixed with oxygen in the air. All blood exposed to air is red.

1. What color is blood that carries oxygen?   Ⓦ D
   <u>Red</u>

2. What color is blood that carries carbon dioxide?   Ⓦ D
   <u>Almost black</u>

3. What color will blood turn if it is exposed to air?   Ⓦ D
   <u>Red</u>

Compound words, comparisons/figurative language, deductions
Directions: If necessary, read the directions for each part. When students have completed the page, present each item and the answer. Correct any errors.
16   © 2001 SRA/McGraw-Hill. Permission is granted to reproduce for classroom use.

LESSON 9

Name _____

Part 1

For each word on the left, write the letter of its definition on the right.

1. oxygen __d__
2. constructive __h__
3. carbon dioxide __i__
4. predictable __f__
5. verb __g__
6. obtain __a__
7. regulatory __b__
8. modify __e__
9. noun __j__
10. adjective __c__

a. (v.) get
b. (a.) something that regulates
c. (n.) a word that comes before a noun and tells about the noun
d. (n.) a gas that burning things need
e. (v.) change
f. (a.) something that is easy to predict
g. (n.) a word that tells the action that things do
h. (a.) something that is helpful
i. (n.) a gas that burning things produce
j. (n.) a word that names a person, place, or thing

Part 2

Write a word that comes from **digest** or **conclude** in each blank. Then fill in the circle beside **verb, noun,** or **adjective.**

1. What __conclusion__ can you come to about the book?
   ○ verb ● noun ○ adjective

2. The stomach is part of the __digestive__ system.
   ○ verb ○ noun ● adjective

Part 3

Follow the directions.

1. Draw a horizontal line.
2. Draw a line that slants down to the right from the right end of the horizontal line.
3. Draw a curve to represent a muscle that covers the bottom of the horizontal line and attaches to the top end of the slanted line.
4. Circle the line that will move when the muscle pulls.

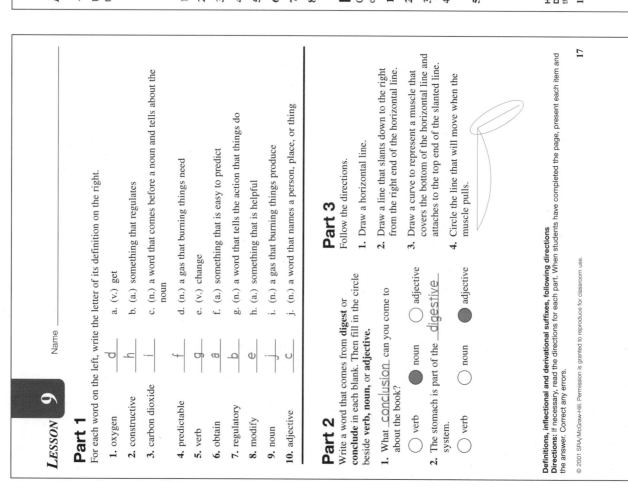

Definitions, inflectional and derivational suffixes, following directions
Directions: If necessary, read the directions for each part. When students have completed the page, present each item and the answer. Correct any errors.
© 2001 SRA/McGraw-Hill. Permission is granted to reproduce for classroom use.

LESSON 9

Name _____

☆ Part 4

Use the homophones from the box to complete the sentences below.

ate	cent	there	blue
eight	sent	their	blew

1. The wind __blew__ my hat off.
2. I __ate__ my breakfast early today.
3. Your backpack is over __there__.
4. We __sent__ the package to Chicago.
5. My neighbor has __eight__ kittens.
6. A penny is one __cent__.
7. Is __their__ house made of brick?
8. The weather forecast is for __blue__ skies.

Part 5

Circle the subject and underline the predicate in each sentence.

1. **Cold, big,** and **old** are adjectives.
2. Bike riding is good exercise.
3. Making friends is part of going to school.
4. The respiratory system brings oxygen to your lungs.
5. Oxygen and carbon dioxide are gases.

Part 6

Write **brain, nerves,** or **spinal cord** in each blank.

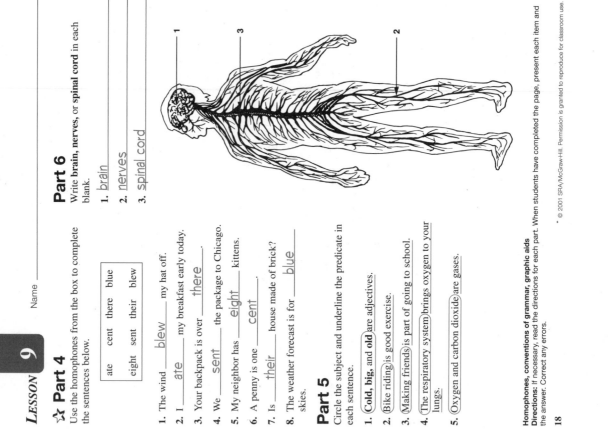

1. brain
2. nerves
3. spinal cord

Homophones, conventions of grammar, graphic aids
Directions: If necessary, read the directions for each part. When students have completed the page, present each item and the answer. Correct any errors.
* © 2001 SRA/McGraw-Hill. Permission is granted to reproduce for classroom use.

Part 1

On the lines below, rewrite the paragraph by combining the sentences that are joined with an underline. If one of the sentences tells **why**, combine the sentences with **because.**

> Betsy was moving to another state. Betsy had three brothers. Her dad got a new job. Her dad is a policeman. Betsy was not happy. She will miss her friends.

Betsy, who had three brothers, was moving to another state. Her dad, who is a policeman, got a new job. Betsy was not happy because she will miss her friends.

Writing/conventions of grammar, homophones
Directions: If necessary, read the directions for each part. When students have completed the page, present each item and the answer. Correct any errors.

19

☆ **Part 2**

Use these homophones to complete the sentences.

> pale pail so sew
> nose knows hair hare

1. She ___knows___ what she wants to eat.
2. His ___nose___ tells him that breakfast is ready.
3. Bobby put sand in the ___pail___ .
4. The sick child looked ___pale___ .
5. The ___hare___ hopped away.
6. He combed his ___hair___ .
7. Dad feels ___so___ happy.
8. He can ___sew___ buttons on his shirt.

Part 3

Tell **two** ways that the things compared are **not** the same. Tell **one** way that the things compared **are** the same.

> **She eats like a bird.**

1. She is not a bird.

2. She is bigger than a bird.

3. They both eat.

Part 4

Shade in each tube that carries dark blood. Tell if each tube is a vein or an artery.

1. ___artery___
2. ___vein___
3. ___vein___
4. ___artery___

Comparisons/figurative language, graphic aids
Directions: If necessary, read the directions for each part. When students have completed the page, present each item and the answer. Correct any errors.

20

LESSON 11

Name _____

☆ Part 1
Fill in the circle next to the correct homophone.

1. The shoe _____ was over yesterday.
   - ○ sail
   - ● sale

2. _____ home is for sale.
   - ○ Hour
   - ● Our

3. A _____ is a kind of fruit.
   - ○ pair
   - ● pear

4. The _____ looked ready to eat.
   - ● meat
   - ○ meet

Part 2
Tell which fact each statement relates to.

1. Blood that carries oxygen is red. _____
2. Blood that carries carbon dioxide is dark. __2__

a. It goes from the heart to the muscles. _____
b. It goes from the muscles to the heart. __2__
c. It is pumped by the heart to all parts of the body. _____

Part 3
Write a word that comes from **reside** or **produce** in each blank. Then fill in the circle beside **verb**, **noun**, or **adjective**.

1. The company stopped _production_.
   - ○ verb ● noun ○ adjective

2. He _resides_ in an old farmhouse.
   - ● verb ○ noun ○ adjective

3. The White House is the _residence_ of the president.
   - ○ verb ● noun ○ adjective

4. Gary has had a _productive_ year growing corn.
   - ○ verb ○ noun ● adjective

Part 4
Tell **two** ways that the things compared are **not** the same.
Tell **one** way that the things compared **are** the same.

Sarah says she feels like a million bucks.

1. Money cannot feel.
2. Sarah is not money.
3. They both are worth a lot.

LESSON 11

Name _____

Part 5
On the lines below, rewrite the paragraph by combining the sentences that are joined with an underline. If one of the sentences tells **why**, combine the sentences with **because**.

> **The digestive system has an important job. The digestive system includes the mouth and stomach. First, your teeth act like sharp blades. The sharp blades cut the food into small bits. The stomach mixes the food with chemicals. The chemicals dissolve the food.**

The digestive system, which includes the mouth and stomach, has an important job. First, your teeth act like sharp blades, which cut the food into small bits. The stomach mixes the food with chemicals, which dissolve the food.

Part 6
Fill in each blank.

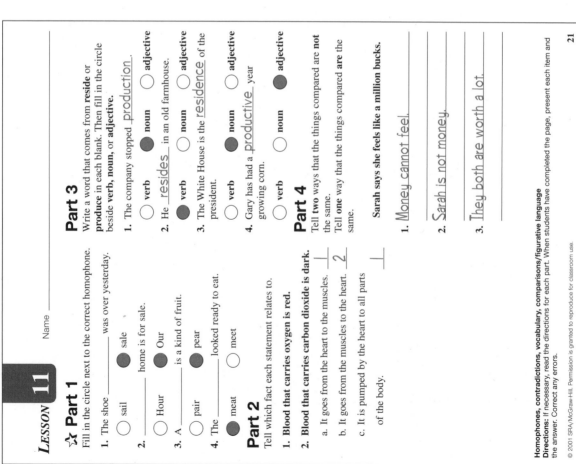

1. mouth
2. esophagus
3. liver
4. stomach
5. small intestine
6. large intestine

Part 1

Write the instructions.

nerves ③ —————— spinal cord ②

① _____

1. (what) Draw a horizontal line.

2. (what and where) Write the words spinal cord to the right of the line.

3. (what and where) Write the word nerves to the left of the line.

☆ Part 2

An **antonym** is a word that means the opposite of another word. Here are some antonym pairs:

hot/cold   in/out   up/down

Fill in the circle beside the antonym for each underlined word.

1. buy   ● sell   ○ redo
2. criticize ○ worry   ● praise
3. over   ● under   ○ beside
4. conclude   ○ make   ● begin
5. construct ● destroy   ○ investigate

Part 3

Write **spinal cord, nerves, brain, central** or **peripheral** in each blank.

1. brain

2. spinal cord

3. nerves _____ nervous system.

1. and 2. central _____ nervous system.

3. peripheral _____ nervous system.

Following directions, antonyms, graphic aids
Directions: If necessary, read the directions for each part. When students have completed the page, present each item and the answer. Correct any errors.

Part 4

Read the story and answer the questions. Circle the **W** if the question is answered by the words in the story, and underline those words. Circle the **D** if the question is answered by a deduction.

> **Your brain is divided into three parts: the cerebrum, the cerebellum, and the medulla. The cerebrum helps you think and feel. The cerebellum controls your muscular system. The medulla controls your digestive, respiratory, and circulatory systems.**

1. List the three parts of your brain.
   Cerebrum, cerebellum, medulla   Ⓦ D

2. What is the medulla's job? Controls digestive, respiratory, and circulatory system   Ⓦ D

3. Which part of your brain works when you feel happy? _____ Cerebrum   W Ⓓ

4. What does the cerebellum do? Controls your muscular system   Ⓦ D

5. Which part controls your digestive system?
   Medulla   Ⓦ D

Part 5

Write a word that comes from **protect** or **criticize** in each blank. Then fill in the circle beside the **verb, noun,** or **adjective.**

1. The woman criticized the cashier for making a mistake.
   ● **verb**   ○ **noun**   ○ **adjective**

2. The dog was very protective of her puppies.
   ○ **verb**   ○ **noun**   ● **adjective**

3. His criticism hurt her feelings.
   ○ **verb**   ● **noun**   ○ **adjective**

4. Some companies require their employees to wear special protection for their jobs.
   ○ **verb**   ● **noun**   ○ **adjective**

Deductions, inflectional and derivational suffixes
Directions: If necessary, read the directions for each part. When students have completed the page, present each item and the answer. Correct any errors.

LESSON 13

Name _____

Part 1

Fill in the blank with the word that has the same meaning as the word or words under the blank.

1. The doctor __examined__ the cat.
(looked at)

2. It is important to __select__ the right class.
(choose)

3. She wants to __obtain__ her diploma.
(get)

Part 2

Write the instructions.

③ trachea

1. (what) Draw a vertical line.

2. (what and where) Draw an oval above the vertical line.

3. (what and where) Write the word trachea below the vertical line.

Part 3

Circle the common part that is at the **beginning** of two sentences. Then combine those sentences with **who** or **which.**

1. The children played in the snow.
   The (snow) lasted a long time.
   The (snow) was good for making snowballs.
   The snow, which was good for making snowballs, lasted a long time.

2. (His boat) is thirty feet long.
   (His boat) belonged to our grandfather.
   My brother likes his sailboat.
   His boat, which belonged to our grandfather, is thirty feet long.

3. (Her teacher) liked to read mysteries.
   Mysteries can be scary.
   (Her teacher) used to be a librarian.
   Her teacher, who used to be a librarian, liked to read mysteries.

4. (The festival) was planned for this weekend.
   This weekend is a holiday weekend.
   (The festival) has lots of food and music.
   The festival, which has lots of food and music, was planned for this weekend.

Vocabulary, following directions, conventions of grammar/writing sentences
Directions: If necessary, read the directions for each part. When students have completed the page, present each item and the answer. Correct any errors.

© 2001 SRA/McGraw-Hill. Permission is granted to reproduce for classroom use.

25

LESSON 13

Name _____

Part 4

Underline the nouns. Draw a line **over** the verbs. Circle the adjectives.

1. Two balloons (floated) toward the blue sky.
2. The happy frog (croaked) loudly.
3. My older brother (wants) a new car.
4. Yesterday the class (planted) two pine trees.

Part 5

Shade in each tube that carries dark blood. Tell if each tube is a **vein** or an **artery.**

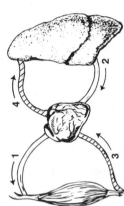

1. artery
2. vein
3. vein
4. artery

☆ Part 6

Look at each word. Choose the correct **antonym** from the box and write it in the space provided.

begin	white	open	down
thick	soft	happy	sleepy

1. hard __soft__
2. end __begin__
3. sad __happy__
4. up __down__
5. thin __thick__
6. black __white__
7. awake __sleepy__
8. shut __open__

Conventions of grammar, graphic aids, antonyms
Directions: If necessary, read the directions for each part. When students have completed the page, present each item and the answer. Correct any errors.

26

© 2001 SRA/McGraw-Hill. Permission is granted to reproduce for classroom use.

LESSON 14

Name _____

Part 1

For each word on the left, write the letter of its definition on the right.

1. protective — e
2. conclude — c
3. nerve — h
4. digestion — g
5. brain — b
6. production — i
7. spinal cord — d
8. conclusive — j
9. criticism — a
10. modified — f

a. (n.) a statement that criticizes
b. (n.) the organ that lets you think and feel
c. (v.) end or figure out
d. (n.) the body part that connects the brain to all parts of the body
e. (a.) that something protects
f. (a.) that something is changed
g. (n.) the act of digesting
h. (n.) a wire in the body that carries messages
i. (n.) something that is produced
j. (a.) that something is true without any doubt

Part 2

Write the instructions

cerebrum | cerebellum
③ ① ②

1. (what) Draw a vertical line.
2. (what and where) Write the word cerebellum to the right of the line.
3. (what and where) Write the word cerebrum to the left of the line.

Part 3

Circle the subject and underline the predicate in each sentence.

1. (Raking leaves) uses many muscles.
2. (The medulla and the cerebrum) are parts of the brain.
3. (Carbon dioxide) is a gas in the air.
4. (Arteries and veins) are parts of the circulatory system.
5. (Brain, nerve, and cerebellum) are all nouns.
6. (To build a house) requires much planning.

Definitions, following directions, conventions of grammar
Directions: Read the directions to each item with the student. Give the student time to respond before going to the next item. When students have completed the page, go over the items and answers. Correct any errors.

© 2001 SRA/McGraw-Hill. Permission is granted to reproduce for classroom use.

27

LESSON 14

Name _____

Part 4

Read the sentences. Fill in the circle for the antonym of the **bold** word.

1. The skyscraper is very **tall.**
   ● short   ○ hot
2. The pancake batter was very **thick.**
   ○ smooth   ● thin
3. It's easy to **go** into the city.
   ● stop   ○ out
4. These cookies are **hard.**
   ○ rough   ● soft
5. In the **evening** we will go for a walk.
   ● morning   ○ noon
6. Do you want to go **before** the movie starts?
   ● after   ○ begin
7. The **bottom** of the boat has a hole in it.
   ○ right   ● top
8. Is this too **short** for you?
   ○ sweet   ● long

Part 5

Write **spinal cord**, **nerves**, **brain**, **central** or **peripheral** in each blank.

1. nerves
2. brain
3. spinal cord

1. peripheral _____ nervous system.
2. and 3. Central _____ nervous system.

Antonyms, graphic aids
Directions: Read the directions to each item with the student. Give the student time to respond before going to the next item. When students have completed the page, go over the items and answers. Correct any errors.

28

© 2001 SRA/McGraw-Hill. Permission is granted to reproduce for classroom use.

LESSON 15

Name _____

Part 1

Fill in each blank

1. trapezius
2. triceps
3. gastrocnemius
4. quadriceps
5. biceps
6. abdominal muscle

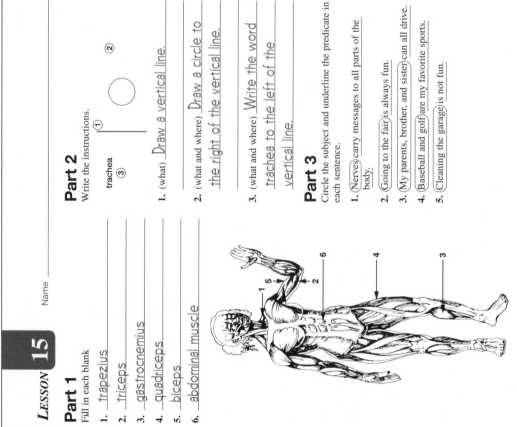

Part 2

Write the instructions.

trachea

① ___ ②

③

1. (what) Draw a vertical line.

2. (what and where) Draw a circle to the right of the vertical line.

3. (what and where) Write the word trachea to the left of the vertical line.

Part 3

Circle the subject and underline the predicate in each sentence.

1. Nerves carry messages to all parts of the body.

2. Going to the fair is always fun.

3. My parents, brother, and sister can all drive.

4. Baseball and golf are my favorite sports.

5. Cleaning the garage is not fun.

LESSON 15

Name _____

Part 4

Underline the common part. Fill in the circle beside the word that combines the sentences correctly. Combine the sentences with that word.

1. The horse stood near the fence.

The horse was brown and white.

○ who ○ because ● which

The horse, which was brown and white, stood near the fence.

2. The computer was broken.

The computer didn't work.

○ who ○ but ● because

The computer didn't work because it was broken.

3. New York is in the East.

Maine is in the East.

○ because ● and ○ who

New York and Maine are in the East.

4. Leslie was sitting on the couch.

Her cat was sitting on the couch.

● and ○ which ○ because

Leslie and her cat were sitting on the couch.

☆ Part 5

- Use a **comma** (,) to separate three or more items listed together in a sentence.
- Use a comma after the words **yes** and **no** if they begin a sentence.

Read the sentences below. Place commas where they belong.

1. You will need glue, paper, scissors, crayons, and a pencil.

2. No, I didn't ask her to come with us.

3. Please bring the milk, eggs, orange juice, and bread from the refrigerator.

4. Yes, it is your turn.

5. The cooler, chairs, beach towels, and toys need to go in the car.

6. Please pack your books, homework assignment, pad, and pencils in your backpack.

7. We want to visit the museum, zoo, beach, and theme park on our vacation.

8. I left my bed unmade, my clothes on the floor, the bathroom messy, and dishes in the sink!

Name _____

Part 1

Write the instructions.

① oxygen ③
②

1. (what) Draw a horizontal line.

2. (what and where) Draw a triangle above the middle of the line.

3. (what and where) Write the word oxygen below the middle of the line.

☆ Part 2

Look at the series of words or phrases in the following sentences. Decide where the commas go and add them.

1. Sandra went to the store and bought apples, oranges, pears, and bananas.

2. On our camping trip we went fishing, hiking, hunting, swimming, and diving.

3. Before you can drive a car you have to take a class, read a book on driving rules, take driving lessons, and pass a test.

Part 3

Rewrite each sentence by moving part of the predicate. The first item is done for you.

1. He went to sleep because he was tired.
   Because he was tired, he went to sleep.

2. Rabbits were hopping in the grass.
   In the grass, rabbits were hopping.

3. He bought a kite when he went to the store.
   When he went to the store, he bought a kite.

4. The grass is wet after it rains.
   After it rains, the grass is wet.

Part 4

Fill in each blank with the word that has the same meaning as the word or words under the blank.

1. A smart person _selects_ friends
   (chooses)
   carefully.

2. Humans _obtain_ oxygen from the air.
   (get)

3. The man wanted to _examine_ the car.
   (look at)

4. The heart _regulates_ how fast the
   (controls)
   blood flows.

31

Name _____

Part 7

Fill in each blank.

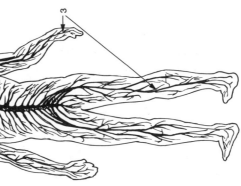

1. spinal cord
2. brain
3. nerves

Part 5

Write **R** for each fact that is **relevant** to what happened. Write **I** for each fact that is **irrelevant** to what happened.

> Last night, **Ken locked his keys in the car and had to call home for help.**

1. Ken is very tall. I

2. Ken keeps a spare key at home. R

3. Ken's car is pink and yellow. I

4. Ken likes to drive. I

Part 6

Tell **two** ways that the things compared are **not** the same.
Tell **one** way that the things compared **are** the same.

The **sun is like a basketball.**

1. The sun is not made of rubber.

2. A basketball is not burning.

3. They are both round.

32

LESSON 17 Name _____

Part 1

a. Underline the common part that is at the **end** of one sentence and the **beginning** of another. Then combine those sentences with **who** or **which**.

b. Circle the common part that is at the **beginning** of two sentences. Then combine those sentences with **who** or **which**.

1. (Some animals) have veins.
   (Some animals) have bones.
   Veins carry blood back to the heart.

   a. Some animals have veins, which carry blood back to the heart.

   b. Some animals, which have bones, have veins.

2. (Sense nerves) carry messages to the brain.
   The brain has three main parts.
   (Sense nerves) let you feel.

   a. Sense nerves carry messages to the brain which has three main parts.

   b. Sense nerves, which let you feel, carry messages to the brain.

Part 2

Fill in each blank.

1. pelvis
2. spine
3. humerus
4. femur
5. ribs
6. skull

Conventions of grammar/writing sentences, graphic aids
Directions: If necessary, read the directions for each part. When students have completed the page, present each item and the answer. Correct any errors.

© 2001 SRA/McGraw-Hill. Permission is granted to reproduce for classroom use.

33

LESSON 17 Name _____

☆ Part 3

Read the sentences below. Place commas where they are needed.

1. Tom likes to play chess, ride his bike, swim, and play basketball.

2. Yes, please pass out the permission slips.

3. Please make your bed, brush your teeth, eat breakfast, and walk the dog.

4. Suzi likes corn and meatloaf for dinner.

5. It's time to close your books, pack your backpacks, and sit down.

6. Let's go to the movies, the video arcade, and the park the next time we come here.

Part 4

Write a word that comes from **predict** or **regulate** in each blank. Then fill in the circle beside **verb, noun,** or **adjective.**

1. The weatherman predicted (predicts) a cold winter.
   ● verb   ○ noun   ○ adjective

2. Her prediction that the cat would come back was correct.
   ○ verb   ● noun   ○ adjective

3. Your cerebellum regulates your muscular system.
   ● verb   ○ noun   ○ adjective

4. The end of the movie was predictable.
   ○ verb   ○ noun   ● adjective

Commas, inflectional and derivational suffixes
Directions: If necessary, read the directions for each part. When students have completed the page, present each item and the answer. Correct any errors.

© 2001 SRA/McGraw-Hill. Permission is granted to reproduce for classroom use.

34

148

Part 1

Use the facts to fill out the form.

> **Facts: Your name is Thomas Jones. You are twelve years old. You have an older sister named Angela and a younger brother named Jeff. Your father is a reporter and your mother is a nurse. Your address is 462 East Broad Street, Columbus, Ohio.**

Instructions:

a. Enter your name on line 2.
b. Write your father's profession on line 6.
c. State your age on line 3.
d. On line 1, write your mother's job.
e. Write your address on line 4.
f. On line 5, write the sentence above that gives information you didn't use in filling out the form.

1. Nurse
2. Thomas Jones
3. Twelve
4. 462 East Broad Street Columbus, Ohio
5. You have an older sister named Angela and a younger brother named Jeff.
6. Reporter

Identifying facts, conventions of grammar/writing sentences
Directions: If necessary, read the directions for each part. When students have completed the page, present each item and the answer. Correct any errors.
© 2001 SRA/McGraw-Hill. Permission is granted to reproduce for classroom use.

Part 2

a. Underline the common part that is at the **end** of one sentence and the **beginning** of another. Then combine those sentences with **who** or **which**.
b. Circle the common part that is at the **beginning** of two sentences. Then combine those sentences with **who** or **which**.

1. (The woman) was very tall.
   (The woman) was watching the football game.

   The football game lasted three hours.

   a. The woman was watching the football game, which lasted three hours.

   b. The woman, who was watching the football game, was very tall.

2. Mars is known as the "Red Planet."
   (Veronica) wants to travel to Mars.

   (Veronica) likes movies about space travel.

   a. Veronica wants to travel to Mars, which is known as the "Red Planet."

   b. Veronica, who likes movies about space travel, wants to travel to Mars.

☆ Part 3

> A **contraction** is a shortened form of two words that are joined together. When the words are joined, one or more letters are left out. An apostrophe is used to show the letters that are left out.
>
> it's = it is   wasn't = was not

Read each pair of sentences. Circle the contraction. Underline the two words it replaces.

1. We do not know how to play.
   We (don't) know how to play.

2. I did not know that Brad could come.
   I (didn't) know that Brad could come.

3. It is supposed to be hot again tomorrow.
   (It's) supposed to be hot again tomorrow.

4. We will read the book after lunch.
   (We'll) read the book after lunch.

Part 4

Tell **two** ways that the things compared are **not** the same.
Tell **one** way that the things compared **are** the same.

The water was like a mirror.

1. Water is not made of glass.
2. Glass is hard.
3. They both reflect things.

Part 5

Write the conclusion of each deduction.

1. Some planets are smaller than Saturn. Mercury is a planet.
   So, maybe Mercury is smaller than Saturn.

2. Every brain has three parts. Marvin has a brain.
   So, Marvin's brain has three parts.

3. Every dog has warm blood. Maynard is a dog.
   So, Maynard has warm blood.

Part 6

Make each statement mean the same thing as the statement in the box.

> **People paid Larry to protect their residences.**

1. Larry was paid to protect people's homes.
2. People gave money to Larry for protecting their residences.
3. ~~Larry~~ People paid ~~people~~ Larry to protect their places of residence.
4. People paid Larry to guard the places where they ~~worked~~ lived.

Contractions comparisons/figurative language, forming generalizations
Directions: If necessary, read the directions for each part. When students have completed the page, present each item and the answer. Correct any errors.

© 2001 SRA/McGraw-Hill. Permission is granted to reproduce for classroom use.

LESSON 19

Name _____

Part 1

For each of the words on the left, write the letter of its definition on the right.

1. irrelevant   d
2. conclude   e
3. nervous system   b
4. digest   g
5. relevant   f
6. examine   a
7. central nervous system   c

a. (v.) look at
b. (n.) the body system that is made up of all the nerves that lead to and from the spinal cord
c. (n.) body system that is made up of the brain and spinal cord
d. (a.) that something does not help to explain what happened
e. (v) end or figure out
f. (a.) that something helps to explain what happened
g. (v.) change food into fuel for the body

Part 2

Underline the contradiction.
Circle the statement it contradicts.

Roger Maris, who played for the New York Yankees, broke Babe Ruth's single-season home-run record by hitting 61 home runs in one season. His record looked unbeatable. In 1998, his record was broken twice. Mark McGuire hit 70 home runs and Sammy Sosa hit 66 in the 1998 season. Batting and pitching records are always falling, but Maris's record will never be broken. Who do you think will be the next person to hit 70 home runs in a single season?

Part 3

Circle the subject and underline the predicate in each sentence. Rewrite each sentence by moving each part of the predicate.

1. (Dogs) often bark when they are scared.
   When they are scared, dogs often bark.

2. (She) ate a large meal at the restaurant.
   At the restaurant, she ate a large meal.

3. (The students) criticized the author after reviewing her novel.
   After reviewing her novel, the students criticized the author.

Definitions, identifying facts, conventions of grammar/writing sentences
Directions: If necessary, read the directions for each part. When students have completed the page, present each item and the answer. Correct any errors.

37

LESSON 19

Name _____

Part 4

Underline the common part. Fill in the circle beside the word that combines the sentences correctly. Combine the sentences with that word.

1. Germany is a country in Europe.
   Italy is a country in Europe.
   ○ which   ● and   ○ because
   Germany and Italy are countries in Europe.

2. Bill wanted to skate.
   Bill borrowed skates.
   ● because   ○ which   ○ but
   Bill borrowed skates because he wanted to skate.

3. Cheetahs run very fast.
   Cheetahs have spots.
   ○ who   ○ because   ● which
   Cheetahs, which run very fast, have spots.

4. Tammy is turning eight today.
   Tammy has black hair.
   ○ because   ● who   ○ which
   Tammy, who has black hair, is turning eight today.

☆ Part 5

Draw a line from the two words to the contraction.

1. I will .... don't
2. she will .... they'll
3. he will .... it'll
4. we will .... I'll
5. they will .... didn't
6. it will .... she'll
7. do not .... we'll
8. did not .... he'll

Conventions of grammar/writing sentences, contractions
Directions: If necessary, read the directions for each part. When students have completed the page, present each item and the answer. Correct any errors.

38

150

LESSON 20 Name _____

Part 1
Circle the subject and underline the predicate in each sentence. Rewrite each sentence by moving part of the predicate.

1. (Your cousin) broke her leg when she fell off her bike.
   When she fell off her bike, your cousin broke her leg.

2. (My father and brother) eat cereal in the morning.
   In the morning, my father and brother eat cereal.

Part 2

② relevant ① ③ irrelevant

1. (what) Draw a triangle.
2. (what and where) Write the word relevant to the left of the triangle.
3. (what and where) Write the word irrelevant underneath the triangle.

Part 3
Use the facts to fill out the form.

> **Facts: Your name is Sara Jensen. You are forty-five years old. You want to buy a house. You are the president of a steel company. You make $150,000 per year. You have two children and a husband named Zeke. Your address is 154 S. Toledo Street, Pittsburgh, Pennsylvania.**

Instructions:
a. Enter your husband's name on line 2.
b. State your age on line 4.
c. On line 3, tell what you want to purchase.
d. Write your full name, last name first, on line 1.
e. Write your address on line 5.
f. On line 6, write the second sentence above that gives information you didn't use in filling out the form.

1. Jensen, Sara
2. Zeke
3. A house
4. Forty-five
5. 154 S. Toledo Street Pittsburgh, Pennsylvania
6. You make $150,000 per year.

Conventions of grammar/writing sentences, writing instructions, identify facts
Directions: If necessary, read the directions for each part. When students have completed the page, present each item and the answer. Correct any errors.
© 2001 SRA/McGraw-Hill. Permission is granted to reproduce for classroom use.
39

LESSON 20 Name _____

Part 4
a. Underline the common part that is at the **end** of one sentence and the **beginning** of another. Then combine those sentences with **who** or **which**.
b. Circle the common part that is at the **beginning** of two sentences. Then combine those sentences with **who** or **which**.

1. (The brain) is the most complex organ in the nervous system.
   (The brain) is part of the nervous system. The nervous system is the system of nerves in the body.
   a. The brain is part of the nervous system, which is the system of nerves in the body.
   b. The brain, which is part of the nervous system, is the most complex organ in the body.

2. (Sam) is a zookeeper.
   A zookeeper feeds and cares for animals at a zoo.
   (Sam) is my older brother.
   a. Sam is a zookeeper, who feeds and cares for animals at the zoo.
   b. Sam, who is my older brother, is a zookeeper.

Part 5
Fill in each blank with the word that has the same meaning as the word or words under the blank.

1. The mechanic modified his car to (changed) make the engine run quietly.
2. Carpenters construct many different (build) types of buildings.
3. The new law is intended to regulate (control) the purchase of cars from foreign countries.
4. Scoliosis is a disease that affects the spinal cord (body part that connects the brain to all parts of the body)

☆ Part 6
Rewrite the underlined word as a contraction.
1. There is not enough paper. Isn't
2. It is time for us to leave. It's
3. I will be leaving soon. I'll
4. Here is some money for lunch. Here's

Conventions of grammar/writing sentences, context clues, contractions
Directions: If necessary, read the directions for each part. When students have completed the page, present each item and the answer. Correct any errors.
40
© 2001 SRA/McGraw-Hill. Permission is granted to reproduce for classroom use.

151

LESSON 21   Name _____

Part 1

Write **R** for each fact that is **relevant** to what happened. Write **I** for each fact that is **irrelevant** to what happened.

> **Sheryl played the trumpet in the marching band.**

1. She has blond hair.
2. She is twenty-four years old.
3. Oranges are Sheryl's favorite fruit.
4. She likes to march with the band.   R

Part 2

Circle the subject and underline the predicate in each sentence. Rewrite each sentence by moving part of the predicate.

1. (Evan and his sister) play tennis at school.
   At school, Evan and his sister play tennis.

2. (Tina's mother) soaked her feet when she went home.
   When she went home, Tina's mother soaked her feet.

3. (Mr. Marek) consumed chicken in a restaurant.
   In a restaurant, Mr. Marek consumed chicken.

Part 3

a. Underline the common part that is at the **end** of one sentence and the **beginning** of another. Then combine those sentences with **who** or **which**.
b. Circle the common part that is at the **beginning** of two sentences. Then combine those sentences with **who** or **which**.

1. (Apples) are good for you.
   (Apples) are ready to eat in the fall.
   The fall is my favorite season.
   a. Apples are ready to eat in the fall, which is my favorite season.
   b. Apples, which are good for you, are ready to eat in the fall.

2. Henry has worked in construction for many years.
   (Burt) agreed to build a house with Henry.
   (Burt) has never built a house before.
   a. Burt agreed to build a house with Henry, who has worked in construction for many years.
   b. Burt, who has never built a house before, agreed to build a house with Henry.

LESSON 21   Name _____

Part 4

Use the facts to fill out the form.

> **Facts: Your name is Molly Jones. You are thirty-six years old. You are a college history teacher. You want the job of head tour guide at the Grand Canyon. Your husband is a third grade teacher. You have written many books about the Grand Canyon. Your address is 4656 Canyon Drive, Phoenix, Arizona.**

Instructions:

a. State your age on line 3.
b. Write your address on line 2.
c. Write your full name, last name first, on line 1.
d. On line 6, state your current profession.
e. State the topic of the books you have written on line 5.
f. State the job you are seeking on line 7.
g. On line 4, write the sentence above that gives information you didn't use in filling out the form.

1. Jones, Molly
2. 4656 Canyon Drive
   Phoenix, Arizona
3. Thirty-six
4. Your husband is a third grade teacher.
5. The Grand Canyon
6. College history teacher
7. Head tour guide at the Grand Canyon

☆ Part 5

> A **synonym** is a word that means almost the same thing as another word.
> **Examples:**   **small/little**   **home/house**

Use the words in the box below to write a synonym for each word.

gift	below	right	new
road	shut	single	enjoy

1. one   single
2. present   gift
3. like   enjoy
4. street   road
5. correct   right
6. under   below
7. fresh   new
8. close   shut

Part 1

Circle the subject and underline the predicate in each sentence. Rewrite each sentence by moving part of the predicate.

1. (Mary) walks three miles to school every day.
   Every day, Mary walks three
   miles to school.

2. (Two frogs) ate flies by the pond.
   By the pond, two frogs ate flies.

3. (They) found a marble under the bed.
   Under the bed, they found a
   marble.

4. (My best friend's mother) saw a shooting star last night.
   Last night, my best friend's
   mother saw a shooting star.

5. (He) reads comic books for fun.
   For fun, he reads comic books.

☆ Part 2

Match the words in Column 1 with their **synonyms** in Column 2.

Column 1   Column 2

1. find   idea
2. fasten   locate
3. fearful   enjoy
4. thought   hook
5. boring   limb
6. branch   dull
7. like   scared
8. car   leave
9. close   auto
10. go   shut

Conventions of grammar/subjects and predicates, synonyms
Directions: If necessary, read the directions for each part. When students have completed the page, present each item and the answer. Correct any errors.

© 2001 SRA/McGraw-Hill. Permission is granted to reproduce for classroom use.

43

Part 3

Read the story and answer the questions. Write **W** after each question that is answered by words in the story, and underline those words. Write **D** after each question that is answered by a deduction.

> Diamonds and coal are made of the same mineral. The mineral that diamonds and coal share is called carbon. Diamonds are used for jewelry, are very hard, and can cut every other material in the world. A diamond is many times more valuable than coal. Coal is used in industry, but it does not have the physical beauty of diamonds.

1. What mineral makes diamonds and coal?
   Carbon (W)

2. Jane had a piece of coal and a diamond. She lost one of them and was very upset. Which one did she lose? The diamond (D)

3. Can a diamond be used to cut a piece of glass?
   Yes (D)

Part 4

Write **R** for each fact that is **relevant** to what happened. Write **I** for each fact that is **irrelevant** to what happened.

> Michael bought a new pair of running shoes.

1. He joined the track team.   R
2. Michael likes to run.   R
3. His sister does not wear shoes.   I
4. He has red running shorts.   I
5. Michael has outgrown his old pair of shoes.   R

Part 5

~~This~~ word means ~~an object that is changed:~~ modified
    modify

1. Cross out the words that tell what this word means.

2. Over the words you crossed out, print the word that means **that an object is changed.**

3. At the end of the sentence, print the verb this word comes from.

4. Circle the adjectives.

Deductions, main idea/relevant and irrelevant details, root words/following directions
Directions: If necessary, read the directions for each part. When students have completed the page, present each item and the answer. Correct any errors.

44

© 2001 SRA/McGraw-Hill. Permission is granted to reproduce for classroom use.

LESSON 23   Name _____

Part 1

Complete the analogies.

1. Tell what part of speech each word is.

Consumer is to ___noun___ as **digestion** is to ___noun___.

2. Tell what verb each word comes from.

Consumer is to ___consume___ as **digestion** is to ___digest___.

3. Tell what ending each word has.

Consumer is to ___-er___ as **digestion** is to ___-ion___.

Part 2

Follow the directions.

1. Draw a horizontal line from left to right.
2. Draw a vertical line of the same length on the right and left ends of the first line.
3. Draw a horizontal line between the two vertical lines.
4. Below the top horizontal line, write the verb that means **look at.**

[examine]

Part 3

Underline the common part. Combine the contradictory sentences with **but.** Combine the other sentences with **who** or **which.**

1. Scott cut down those trees.

Those trees are too tall.

Scott cut down those trees, which were too tall.

2. Thomas Edison invented many things.

Thomas Edison was born in Ohio.

Thomas Edison, who was born in Ohio, invented many things.

3. George Washington was the first president of the United States.

The United States now consists of fifty states.

George Washington was the first president of the United States, which now consists of fifty states.

4. Gordon wanted to buy four oranges.

Gordon bought only two oranges.

Gordon wanted to buy four oranges, but he bought only two oranges.

Analogies, following multistep directions, conventions of grammar/writing sentences
Directions: If necessary, read the directions for each part. When students have completed the page, present each item and the answer. Correct any errors.

LESSON 23   Name _____

☆ Part 4

Fill in the circle next to the **synonym** for each underlined word.

1. Debbie tripped and fell on the trail.
   ● path   ○ log   ○ dirt
2. Huge clouds covered the sun.
   ○ little   ● big   ○ dark
3. I peeked around the corner to see the accident.
   ○ jumped   ○ shouted   ● glanced
4. She was excited about going in an airplane.
   ● thrilled   ○ sad   ○ anxious
5. Steve shut the door when he went to school.
   ● closed   ○ locked   ○ kicked
6. Tina likes corn on the cob.
   ○ cooks   ● enjoys   ○ buys
7. Please complete your homework before dinner.
   ○ stop   ○ under   ● finish
8. Do you have a pencil I could use?
   ● own   ○ old   ○ borrow

Part 5

Underline the nouns. Draw a line **over** the adjectives. Circle the verbs.

1. Tom and Roberto are skating on the pond.
2. The man and the woman have been running for ten minutes.
3. The singers sang mostly work songs and love songs.
4. Fred hurt his little toe, and the doctor gave him a big cast.
5. His older brother consumed grapes with his lunch.
6. Her cats liked the mud.

Part 6

Make each statement mean the same thing as the statement in the box.

[Frogs and lizards consume and digest bugs.]

1. Frogs and children eat insects.   lizards / bugs
2. Lizards and frogs eat snakes.   digest
3. Lizards and frogs consume and produce insects.   insects
4. Frogs and lizards eat bears.

Synonyms, conventions of grammar, forming generalizations
Directions: If necessary, read the directions for each part. When students have completed the page, present each item and the answer. Correct any errors.

Part 1

For each word on the left write the letter of its definition on the right.

1.	obtain	g	a. (n.) something that consumes
2.	conclusive	f	b. (n.) something that is constructed
3.	modification	e	c. (a.) that something can be consumed
4.	consumer	a	d. (n.) a nerve that lets you move
5.	motor nerve	d	e. (n.) a change
6.	consumable	c	f. (a.) something that is true without any doubt
7.	sense nerve	h	g. (v.) get
8.	construction	b	h. (n.) a nerve that lets you feel

Part 2

Underline the contradiction. Circle the statement it contradicts. Tell **why** the underlined statement contradicts the circled statement.

> In 1522, the remaining members of Ferdinand Magellan's crew arrived in Spain. Spain looked good to them. Five ships had started the trip, but only one ship returned. The crew had acquired many different spices on the journey. People in Spain paid a lot of money for the spices, since they were very rare. The king and queen of Spain were sad that only three of the ships survived the journey.

Only one of the ships returned safely, not three.

Part 3

Tell **two** ways that the things compared are **not** the same. Tell **one** way that the things compared **are** the same.

> That cupcake is like a rock.

1. Rocks are not made of flour.
2. We don't eat rocks.
3. Both the cupcake and the rock are hard.

Definitions, identifying clues that allow one to find contradictions, comparisons/figurative language
Directions: If necessary, read the directions for each part. When students have completed the page, present each item and the answer. Correct any errors.

© 2001 SRA/McGraw-Hill. Permission is granted to reproduce for classroom use.

47

Part 4

Write a word that comes from **obtain** in each blank. Then fill in the circle beside **verb, noun,** or **adjective.**

1. I plan on obtaining my driver's license this summer.
   ● verb ○ noun ○ adjective
2. Tara obtained a newspaper from one of her friends.
   ● verb ○ noun ○ adjective
3. Where did you obtain such a beautiful painting?
   ● verb ○ noun ○ adjective

☆ Part 5

> **Alphabetical order** is the order of the letters in the alphabet. To put words in alphabetical order, look at the first letters of each word.

Write each set of words in alphabetical order.

a. oar   canoe   paddle

1. canoe
2. oar
3. paddle

b. pole   price   pump

1. pole
2. price
3. pump

Part 6

Use the rule to answer the questions.

> **The more meat you eat, the more protein you get.**

1. Brian eats three hamburgers a day. Terry eats two hamburgers a day.
   a. Who gets more protein? Brian
   b. How do you know? Because he eats more hamburgers
2. Sally gets thirty grams of protein a day. Kathy gets seventy grams of protein a day.
   a. Who eats more meat? Kathy
   b. How do you know? Because meat has protein
3. Jack eats three pounds of meat a week. Eric eats five pounds of meat a week.
   a. Who gets more protein? Eric
   b. How do you know? Because meat has protein

Inflectional suffixes, alphabetical order, making assumptions
Directions: If necessary, read the directions for each part. When students have completed the page, present each item and the answer. Correct any errors.

48

© 2001 SRA/McGraw-Hill. Permission is granted to reproduce for classroom use.

LESSON 25   Name _____

☆ Part 1

Read the words below. Number the terms in each group in alphabetical order.

1. adjectives   _1_
   nouns   _4_
   verbs   _8_
   adverbs   _2_
   pronouns   _6_
   apostrophes   _3_
   possessives   _5_
   tenses   _7_

2. capitalization   _2_
   punctuation   _7_
   abbreviations   _1_
   initials   _6_
   quotes   _8_
   commas   _4_
   closing   _3_
   greeting   _5_

Part 2

Underline the common part. Combine the sentences with who or which.

1. Greg saw a giant apple on his desk.
   Greg has red hair.
   Greg, who has red hair, saw a giant apple on his desk.

2. The vena cava is the biggest vein in your body.
   The vena cava carries no oxygen.
   The vena cava, which carries no oxygen, is the biggest vein in your body.

3. Linda and Jim went to see a movie.
   Jim did not like the movie.
   Linda and Jim went to see a movie, which Jim did not like.

4. Misty was sad.
   Misty got her hair cut.
   Misty, who got her hair cut, was sad.

Alphabetical order, conventions of grammar/writing sentences
Directions: If necessary, read the directions for each part. When students have completed the page, present each item and the answer. Correct any errors.

© 2001 SRA/McGraw-Hill. Permission is granted to reproduce for classroom use.

49

LESSON 25   Name _____

Part 3

Draw in the arrows. Shade in each tube that carries dark blood. Tell if each tube is a vein or an artery.

1. vein
2. artery
3. artery
4. vein

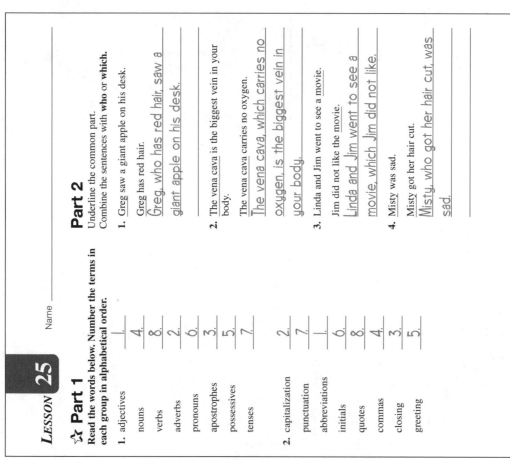

Part 4

Circle the subject and underline the predicate in each sentence. Rewrite each sentence by moving the predicate.

1. Tom and Roberto went skating last night.
   Last night, Tom and Roberto went skating.

2. The man and the woman have been running for ten minutes.
   For ten minutes, the man and the woman have been running.

3. Doug was happy because he made the team.
   Because he made the team, Doug was happy.

Part 5

Write a word that comes from **explain** in each blank. Then fill in the circle beside **verb, noun,** or **adjective.**

1. She is explaining to the doctor what hurts.
   ● verb   ○ noun   ○ adjective

2. Her explanation was easy to understand.
   ○ verb   ● noun   ○ adjective

3. Don wrote an explanatory letter to the city council.
   ○ verb   ○ noun   ● adjective

Graphic aids, conventions of grammar/writing sentences, inflectional/derivational suffixes
Directions: If necessary, read the directions for each part. When students have completed the page, present each item and the answer. Correct any errors.

© 2001 SRA/McGraw-Hill. Permission is granted to reproduce for classroom use.

50

Name _____

Part 1

Write the middle part of each deduction.

1. Giant apes like to eat bananas.

   Gog is a giant ape.

   Gog likes to eat bananas.

   So, Gog likes to eat bananas.

2. Professional baseball players make a great deal of money.

   He is a professional baseball

   player.

   So, he makes a great deal of money.

3. People who eat oranges get vitamin C.

   Sheryl eats oranges.

   So, Sheryl gets vitamin C.

Part 2

Tell which fact each statement relates to.

> 1. **Tom wants his quadriceps bigger.**
> 2. **Ted was breathing the clean mountain air.**

1. The oxygen went into his lungs. _2_

2. He wants to work on a four-headed muscle. _1_

3. The muscle covers the back of his femur. _1_

Part 3

Underline the common part. Fill in the circle beside the word that combines the sentences correctly. Combine the sentences with that word.

1. Dolphins are not fish.

   Dolphins live in the water.

   ○ but ● which ○ because

   Dolphins, which live in the water,

   are not fish.

2. Matthew is an experienced babysitter.

   Matthew has two younger sisters.

   ○ because ○ which ● who

   Matthew, who has two younger

   sisters, is an experienced

   babysitter.

3. Molly didn't watch the movie.

   The movie was very scary.

   ○ who ● because ○ and

   Molly didn't watch the movie

   because it was very scary.

4. Bologna is my favorite sandwich.

   Today I am eating a cheese sandwich.

   ○ who ● but ○ which

   Bologna is my favorite sandwich,

   but today I am eating a cheese

   sandwich.

Directions: If necessary, read the directions for each part. When students have completed the page, present each item and the answer. Correct any errors.

51

Name _____

Part 4

Fill in each blank.

1. spine
2. humerus
3. skull
4. ribs
5. femur
6. pelvis

☆ Part 5

Number the words in each group in **alphabetical order**. The first one is done for you.

1. whale, where, weary, water
   3   4   2   1

2. school, sailor, second, safety
   3   2   4   1

3. recess, rose, ring, reminder
   1   4   3   2

4. earth, earn, ease, each
   3   2   4   1

5. mist, mite, mixture, mischief
   2   3   4   1

Part 6

Tell whether each action is controlled by a **sense** nerve or a **motor** nerve. Fill in the correct circle.

1. "Close eyes."   ○ sense   ● motor
2. "Nod head."   ○ sense   ● motor
3. "See light."   ● sense   ○ motor
4. "Wrist hurts." ● sense   ○ motor

Directions: If necessary, read the directions for each part. When students have completed the page, present each item and the answer. Correct any errors.

52

158

Part 1

Write the conclusion of each deduction.

1. Things need oxygen in order to burn.

   Candles burn.

   So, candles need oxygen in
   order to burn.

2. Containers hold things.

   A cup is a container.

   So, a cup holds things.

3. Things made from milk contain vitamin D.

   Cheese is made from milk.

   So, cheese contains Vitamin D.

Part 2

Make up a simile for each item.

1. Her hair is soft and shiny.

   (Her hair is like silk.)

2. His hair is extremely white.

   (His hair is like snow.)

3. My hands were cold.

   (My hands were like ice.)

Part 3

Write a word that comes from **consume** or **modify** in each blank. Then fill in the circle beside the word. Circle **verb, noun,** or **adjective.**

1. I assume that vegetables are Consumable, because many people eat them.

   ○ verb   ○ noun   ● adjective

2. Charles modified his bike so he would have a better chance of winning.

   ● verb   ○ noun   ○ adjective

3. Car manufacturers are trying to impress consumers .

   ○ verb   ● noun   ○ adjective

Part 4

Circle the subject and underline the predicate in each sentence. Rewrite each sentence by moving the predicate.

1. (The price of grapes) will rise after the drought.

   After the drought, the price of
   grapes will rise.

2. (Blood that is almost black) carries carbon dioxide throughout the body.

   Throughout the body, blood that is
   almost black carries carbon dioxide.

3. (Tabitha's ice-cream shop) buys fifty gallons of milk each week.

   Each week, Tabitha's ice-cream
   shop buys fifty gallons of milk.

Evaluate statements, figurative language/simile, conventions of grammar/writing sentences
Directions: If necessary, read the directions for each part. When students have completed the page, present each item and the answer. Correct any errors.

© 2001 SRA/McGraw-Hill. Permission is granted to reproduce for classroom use.

53

Part 5

Write the instructions.

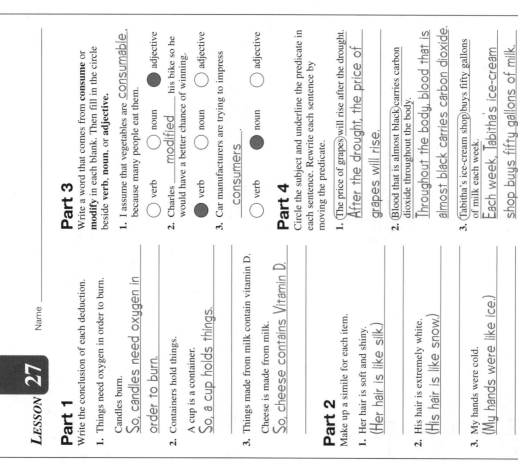

1. (what) Draw a rectangle.

2. (what and where) Write the word consume above the rectangle.

3. (what and where) Write the word digest below the rectangle.

☆ Part 6

- An **abbreviation** is the shortened form of a word.
- Use a capital letter to begin an abbreviation for a title of respect or an abbreviation for the name of a place. Use a period at the end of these abbreviations.

  Examples: Ms., Mrs., Dr., Short St.

Write the names correctly.

1. e m Thomas   E. M. Thomas

2. ms t crotty   Ms. T. Crotty

3. Princeton road   Princeton Rd.

Part 7

Underline the common part. Fill in the circle beside the word that combines the sentences correctly. Combine the sentences with that word.

1. The train was moving slowly.

   The car was moving slowly.

   ○ who   ● and   ○ because

   The train and the car were
   moving slowly.

2. Carla's story was bad.

   Dan read Carla's story.

   ○ because   ● which   ○ who

   Dan read Carla's story, which was
   bad.

3. Many birds don't like cold weather.

   Many birds fly south before winter starts.

   ○ who   ● because   ○ which

   Many birds fly south before
   winter starts because they don't
   like cold weather.

4. Shanece is the smartest student in the class.

   Shanece is my best friend.

   ● who   ○ but   ○ which

   Shanece, who is my best friend,
   is the smartest student in the
   whole class.

Writing directions, abbreviations, conventions of grammar/writing sentences
Directions: If necessary, read the directions for each part. When students have completed the page, present each item and the answer. Correct any errors.

54

© 2001 SRA/McGraw-Hill. Permission is granted to reproduce for classroom use.

Part 1

Read the story and answer the questions.
Write **W** after each question that is answered by words in the story, and underline those words.
Write **D** after each question that is answered by a deduction.

> Before Bill made a kite, he got a book on kite building and studied it for a long time. The first kite Bill constructed was a Chinese snake kite. It had a tail that was ten meters long. The tail got tangled up in a tree, and Bill lost the kite. So he made a box kite. It was the highest-flying kite he made. It went up over two thousand meters. Sadly, the string broke and Bill never found the kite. The last kite Bill made was a diving kite. He could make it dive by letting go of the string. To pull the kite out of a dive, Bill pulled hard on the string.

1. What kind of kite was Bill's second kite?
   A box kite (W)

2. How many kites did Bill build? Three (D)

3. Why couldn't Bill get his kite out of the tree?
   The tail was tangled. (W)

Part 2

Fill in each blank with the word that has the same meaning as the word under the blank.

1. Before the game started, Shawn needed to
   obtain a baseball bat.
   (get)

2. Terrance consumed the whole pizza.
   (ate)

3. The factory produces cars and boats.
   (makes)

Part 3

Write **R** for each fact that is **relevant** to what happened. Write **I** for each fact that is **irrelevant** to what happened.

> Sara made a big salad and ate it outside in the warm sun.

1. Sara lives in Oregon. | I
2. Many of Sara's friends like sports. | I
3. She was very hungry. | R
4. Sara loves to eat lettuce. | R
5. Sara was with her dog Sparky. | I
6. Sara's brother is named Martin. | I

Deductions, context clues, distinguishing between relevant and irrelevant details
Directions: If necessary, read the directions for each part. When students have completed the page, present each item and the answer. Correct any errors.

55

☆ Part 4

- Use capital letters to begin **abbreviations** for days of the week. Use periods at the end of the abbreviations.

  Examples: Sun., Mon., Wed., Thurs., Sat.

- Use capital letters to begin abbreviations for the months of the year.

  Examples: Jan., Feb., Apr., Aug., Nov.

Write the abbreviations for the days and the months. Use capital letters and periods where they are needed.

1. September   Sept.
2. Thursday   Thurs.
3. November   Nov.
4. Monday   Mon.
5. Friday   Fri.
6. October   Oct.
7. January   Jan.
8. December   Dec.
9. Wednesday   Wed.
10. February   Feb.

Part 5

Underline the common part. Fill in the circle beside the word that combines the sentences correctly. Combine the sentences with that word.

1. Cats purr when they are eating.
   Cats purr when they are sleeping.
   ○ but   ● and   ○ because
   Cats purr when they are eating and sleeping.

2. Rick is going to golf with Stone.
   Stone is my brother.
   ○ because   ○ which   ● who
   Rick is going to golf with Stone, who is my brother.

3. Winter is my favorite season.
   I like to ski in the winter.
   ○ who   ● because   ○ but
   Winter is my favorite season, because I like to ski.

Abbreviations, conventions of grammar/writing sentences
Directions: If necessary, read the directions for each part. When students have completed the page, present each item and the answer. Correct any errors.

56

LESSON 29

Name _____

Part 1

For each word on the left write the letter of its definition on the right.

1. arteries   _e._   a. (v.) use up or eat

2. capillaries   _f._   b. (n.) the tubes that carry blood back to the heart

3. circulatory system   _g._   c. (v.) guard

4. consume   _a._   d. (v.) make something easier to understand

5. digestion   _j._   e. (n.) the tubes that carry blood away from the heart

6. explain   _d._   f. (n.) the very small tubes that connect arteries and veins

7. heart   _i._   g. (n.) the body system that moves blood around the body

8. veins   _b._   h. (n.) a statement that tells how things are the same

9. protect   _c._   i. (n.) the pump that moves the blood

10. simile   _h._   j. (n.) the act of digesting

Part 2

Follow the directions.

1. Draw a horizontal line.

2. Draw a vertical line through the middle of the horizontal line.

3. Draw a second vertical line at the right end of the horizontal line.

4. To the left of the first vertical line, write the verb that means **guard.**

protect ————————

Part 3

Tell whether each action is controlled by a **sense** nerve or a **motor** nerve. Fill in the correct circle.

1. "Slap wall."   ◯ sense   ● motor

2. "Watch movie."   ● sense   ◯ motor

3. "Hair is wet."   ● sense   ◯ motor

4. "Open mouth."   ◯ sense   ● motor

5. "Smell grass."   ● sense   ◯ motor

57

LESSON 29

Name _____

Part 4

Rewrite the abbreviations. Use capital letters and periods where needed.

1. aug   Aug.

2. smith rd   Smith Rd.

3. mr c lee   Mr. C. Lee

4. fri   Fri.

5. dr a roberts   Dr. A. Roberts

6. ms n lincoln   Ms. N. Lincoln

7. apr   Apr.

Part 5

Write a word that comes from **manufacture** in each blank. Fill in the circle beside **noun, verb,** or **adjective.**

1. My grandfather __manufactures__ candy.

   ◯ noun   ● verb   ◯ adjective

2. He has been __manufacturing__ candy for twenty years.

   ◯ noun   ● verb   ◯ adjective

3. When I grow up, I want to be a candy __manufacturer__, too.

   ● noun   ◯ verb   ◯ adjective

Part 6

Read the story and answer the questions. Write **W** after each question that is answered by words in the story, and underline those words.

Write **D** after each question that is answered by a deduction.

> **The pulmonary vein is part of the circulatory system. It carries blood from the lungs to the heart. It is the only vein in the body that carries oxygen. It is also one of the biggest veins in the body.**

1. What system does the pulmonary vein belong to? Circulatory system (W)

2. What gas do other veins carry? Carbon dioxide (D)

3. How does blood get from the lungs to the heart? Through the pulmonary vein (W)

58

Part 1

Write a word that comes from **protect** in each blank. Fill in the correct circle beside **noun**, **verb**, or **adjective**.

1. A body guard is a person who <u>protects</u> another person.

○ noun ● verb ○ adjective

2. A hat will give <u>protection</u> from the cold.

● noun ○ verb ○ adjective

3. Catchers wear <u>protective</u> gear to help them avoid being injured.

○ noun ○ verb ● adjective

Part 2

Tell **two** ways that the things compared are **not** the same.
Tell **one** way that the things compared **are** the same.

| The wind howled like a wolf. |

1. The wind is not an animal.

2. Wolves are not made only of moving air.

3. Both can howl.

Part 3

Underline the contradiction. Circle the statement it contradicts. Tell **why** the underlined statement contradicts the circled statement.

Jerome was a paper clip manufacturer. (Every day he woke up at 6 A.M. and went straight to his factory.) He made sure that the factory workers were doing their jobs. Jerome liked his factory, which is why he went to work at 10 A.M. every day to talk to the employees. His workers were happy because he paid them good salaries.

If Jerome got up at 6 A.M. and went straight to work, he would be there before 10 A.M.

Part 4

Circle the subject and underline the predicate in each sentence. Rewrite each sentence by moving the predicate.

1. (Henry Ford) started the Ford Motor Company in 1903.

In 1903, Henry Ford started the Ford Motor Company.

2. (Louis and his sister) came home on a cold winter night.

On a cold winter night, Louis and his sister came home.

59

Part 5

Read the story and answer the questions.
Write **W** after each question that is answered by words in the story, and underline those words.
Write **D** after each question that is answered by a deduction.

The man came home at 5:30 on a cold winter night. He started a fire in his fireplace. By 6:00 the room was warm, so he took off his coat and hat. Right then he noticed that the room was filled with smoke. He went outside and noticed that no smoke was coming out of the chimney. The man became very angry.

1. Was the room **hot** or **cold** when the man got home? <u>cold</u> (D)

2. Was the chimney working properly?
No (D)

3. How long did it take the room to heat up?
30 Minutes (D)

4. How did the man feel about the chimney?
Angry (W)

☆ Part 6

- **A pronoun** is a word that takes the place of a noun.
- Pronouns that take the place of singular nouns are I, me, you, he, him, she, her, and it.
  Example: **Bill** ate slowly. **He** ate slowly.
- Pronouns that take the place of plural nouns are we, us, you, they, and them.
  Example: The ice cream is for **them.**

Choose the correct pronoun in ( ) to take the place of the underlined noun. Then rewrite the sentence.

1. Mrs. Chapman made popcorn for the class. (She, They)
She made popcorn for the class.

2. Students love to eat popcorn. (She, They)
They love to eat popcorn.

3. Ron put salt on his popcorn. (He, They)
He put salt on his popcorn.

162

Part 1

Circle the subject and underline the predicate in each sentence. Rewrite each sentence by moving the predicate.

1. (Jaime) had to get a loan to pay for his new car.
   To pay for his new car, Jaime had
   to get a loan.

2. (Fresh fruits and vegetables) are expensive compared to canned fruits and vegetables.
   Compared to canned fruits and
   vegetables, fresh fruits and
   vegetables are expensive.

3. (Your cousin Evan) sold his house a week ago.
   A week ago, your cousin Evan
   sold his house.

Part 2

Make each statement mean the same thing as the statement in the box.

> **Simone worked hard and had a productive day.**

1. Simone worked hard and finished many things.
   was productive

2. Simone failed because she worked hard.
   worked hard

3. Simone spent a productive day working hard.
   worked hard

4. Simone was lazy and had a productive day.

Part 3

Follow the directions.

1. Draw a rectangle.

2. Draw an arrow outside the rectangle that points to the top left corner of the rectangle.

3. Draw an arrow outside the rectangle that points to the top right corner of the rectangle.

4. Inside the rectangle, write the noun that means **something that explains**.

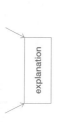

explanation

Part 4

Write a word that comes from **explain** or **predict** in each blank. Fill in the correct circle beside **noun**, **verb**, or **adjective**.

1. My mother __explained__ how to change the oil in the car.
   ○ noun ● verb ○ adjective

2. What is your __prediction__ will win the game?
   ● noun ○ verb ○ adjective for who

3. Could you __explain__ how to make a cake?
   ○ noun ● verb ○ adjective

Conventions of grammar/writing sentences, forming generalizations, following directions, context clues
Directions: If necessary, read the directions for each part. When students have completed the page, present each item and the answer. Correct any errors.

Part 5

Underline the contradiction. Circle the statement it contradicts. Tell **why** the underlined statement contradicts the circled statement.

> Last summer, everyone in Mudville wanted a pair of sandals. Mrs. Laredo ran the only shoe store in the entire town. Mrs. Laredo bought many pairs of sandals. (For each pair of sandals that Mrs. Laredo sold, her store made a profit of ten dollars.) As soon as people heard that Mrs. Laredo was selling sandals, they rushed over to the store to buy a pair. By the end of the first day, Mrs. Laredo had sold six pairs of sandals, for a profit of $300. The store ran out of sandals by the end of the week.

Mrs. Laredo's store made $10 per
pair sold, or $60.

Part 6

Make up a simile for each item.

1. The man cried for a long time.
   (The man cried like a baby.)

2. Inside the cave, it was very dark.
   (Inside the cave, it was dark as night.)

3. My steak was very tough and hard to eat.
   (My steak was like leather.)

Part 7

Combine the sentences with **particularly**.

1. Mexico has pyramids.
   Mexico has many pyramids near Mexico City.
   Mexico has pyramids, particularly near Mexico City.

2. My dad likes to watch football.
   My dad likes to watch college football the most.
   My dad likes to watch football, particularly college football.

3. Terrance is happy.
   Terrance is happiest when it is hot.
   Terrance is happy, particularly when it is hot.

☆ Part 8

Underline the pronouns in the following sentences. Circle the noun or nouns that each pronoun replaces.

1. (Betsy) lost her kitten.

2. (Tim) placed his book on the table.

3. (Marisa) saw her bus coming down the street.

4. It was Jerry's (book) that was on the floor.

5. (Jeff's) mother told him to come straight home from school.

Identifying contradictions, figurative language/similes, conventions of grammar/writing sentences, pronouns
Directions: If necessary, read the directions for each part. When students have completed the page, present each item and the answer. Correct any errors.

Part 1

Use the facts to fill out the form.

> Facts: Your name is Zeus Jackson. You are eighteen years old. You are applying to get into State College. Two of your relatives graduated from State College. Chess is your favorite pastime. You are the president of the chess club. Your address is 324 Red Oak Avenue, San Diego, California.

Instructions:

a. State which club you are president of on line 7.
b. State your age on line 5.
c. On line 1, write what your favorite pastime is.
d. Name the college you would like to attend on line 3.
e. On line 4, write your address.
f. Write your full name, last name first, on line 6.
g. Write the sentence above that gives information you didn't use in filling out the form on line 2.

1. Chess
2. Two of your relatives graduated from State College.
3. State College
4. 324 Red Oak Avenue San Diego, California
5. Eighteen
6. Jackson, Zeus
7. The Chess Club

Part 2

Write the instructions.

1. (what and where) (Draw a horizontal line.)

2. (what and where) (Draw a vertical line starting at the left end of the horizontal line and moving upward.)

3. (what and where) (Draw a slanted line that connects the first two lines.)

Part 3

Write a word that comes from **criticize** in each blank. Fill in the correct circle beside **noun**, **verb**, or **adjective**.

1. He quit the team because he couldn't stand the coach's _____ criticism _____ .
   ● noun   ○ verb   ○ adjective

2. Must you _____ criticize _____ everything I do?
   ○ noun   ● verb   ○ adjective

3. The art critic _____ criticized _____ Sheri's new painting.
   ○ noun   ● verb   ○ adjective

Identifying facts, writing instructions, context clues
Directions: If necessary, read the directions for each part. When students have completed the page, present each item and the answer. Correct any errors.

© 2001 SRA/McGraw-Hill. Permission is granted to reproduce for classroom use.

63

☆ Part 4

Use the pronouns in the box below to complete each sentence.

We	they	Our
them	My	your

1. Did _____ your _____ sister get married last summer?

2. _____ My _____ elbow hurt all day at school.

3. Where did _____ they _____ say the coats were?

4. _____ Our _____ favorite cousin is coming for a visit this weekend.

5. I saw _____ them _____ on my way to baseball practice.

6. _____ We _____ went to the museum and the park.

Part 5

Rewrite the paragraph in four sentences on the lines below. If two of the sentences tell **why,** combine the sentences with **because.** If the sentences seem contradictory, combine them with **but.**

> Blue River is the longest river in the county. My house is next to Blue River. I like to swim. I like most to swim in Blue River. Blue River is too deep to swim in right now. There was a bad rainstorm last night. My little brother is afraid of the water and has never gone swimming in the river. My little brother is ten years old.

My house is next to Blue River, which is the longest river in the county. I like to swim, particularly in Blue River. Blue River is too deep to swim in right now because there was a bad rainstorm last night. My little brother, who is ten years old, is afraid of the water and has never gone swimming in the river.

Pronouns, conventions of grammar/writing sentences
Directions: If necessary, read the directions for each part. When students have completed the page, present each item and the answer. Correct any errors.

64   © 2001 SRA/McGraw-Hill. Permission is granted to reproduce for classroom use.

LESSON 33
Name _____

Part 1
Underline the contradiction. Circle the statement it contradicts. Tell why the underlined statement contradicts the circled statement.

(Larry is a big rabbit with short ears.) All of Larry's friends and relatives have big ears. Whenever they see Larry, the other rabbits can't stop from laughing at how funny he looks with a big body and short, little ears. One day, as Larry is hopping through a garden, he hears a cry for help. When he finally finds where the cry is coming from, he sees his friends trapped under a box. Since he is so small, Larry is able to knock the box over and save his friends. Since then, no rabbits laugh at Larry.

Larry is a big rabbit, not a small one.

Part 2
Fill in each blank with the word that has the same meaning as the word or words under the blank.

1. Marvin was very sick and was not able to ___digest___ anything but dry toast.
(change food into fuel for the body)

2. To make things clear, he ___explained___ again.
(made easier to understand)

3. I wear a heavy jacket to ___protect___ me from the cold weather.
(guard)

Part 3
Write the instructions.

1. (what) Draw a horizontal line.
2. (what and where) Draw a triangle above the line.
3. (what and where) Write the word capillaries below the line.

Part 4
Make up a simile for each item.

1. She runs really fast.
(She runs like the wind.)

2. His skin is very pale.
(His skin is white like a ghost.)

3. The fog is very thick.
(The fog is like pea soup.)

4. Her cheeks are very red.
(Her cheeks are like roses.)

Identifying contradictions, context clues, writing instructions, figurative language/similes
Directions: If necessary, read the directions for each part. When students have completed the page, present each item and the answer. Correct any errors.

LESSON 33
Name _____

Part 5
Underline the common part in each sentence. Fill in the circle beside the word that combines the sentences correctly. Combine the sentences with that word.

1. I am eighteen.
I have the right to vote.
○ particularly ○ which ● because
I have the right to vote because I am eighteen.

2. Brazil is in South America.
Portuguese is the official language of Brazil.
● because ○ which ○ who
Portuguese is the official language of Brazil, which is in South America.

3. Jamal likes to go skiing.
Jamal likes to go skiing most in Colorado.
○ who ● particularly ○ which
Jamal likes to go skiing, particularly in Colorado.

4. Anne is a teacher.
Anne does not like students.
○ particularly ● but ○ which
Anne is a teacher, but she does not like students.

☆ Part 6

- A **statement** tells something and ends with a **period**.
  Cody went for a walk.
- A **question** asks something and ends with a **question mark**.
  When will you be done?
- A sentence that shows strong feeling ends with an **exclamation point** and is called an **exclamation**.
  I am so happy for you!

Read each sentence. Write an **S** if it is a statement, a **Q** if it is a question, or an **E** if it is an exclamation.

Q 1. What time is dinner?
E 2. We won the game!
S 3. She likes to travel in the summer.
Q 4. Did you want to see me?
E 5. I can't wait for the party!
Q 6. How do we get to the parade?
S 7. I put my pencils in my desk.
E 8. Watch out for that car!
S 9. It's time to go to bed.
E 10. I want to eat dinner now!

Conventions of grammar/writing sentences, types of sentences
Directions: If necessary, read the directions for each part. When students have competed the page, present each item and the answer. Correct any errors.

Part 1

For each word on the left, write the letter of its definition on the right.

1. manufactured	c	a. (n.)	the tube that brings outside air to the lungs
2. lung	e	b. (v.)	look at
3. select	j	c. (a.)	that something has been made in a factory
4. trachea	a	d. (v.)	make something easier to understand
5. bronchial tubes	g	e. (n.)	a large organ that brings air into contact with the blood
6. conclude	h	f. (n.)	the body system that brings oxygen to the blood
7. reside	i	g. (n.)	the tubes inside the lungs
8. examine	b	h. (v.)	end or figure out
9. respiratory system	f	i. (v.)	live somewhere
10. explain	d	j. (v.)	choose

Part 2

Follow the directions.

1. Draw a vertical line.
2. Draw a large square on the right side of the vertical line.
3. Draw a second vertical line to the right of the large square.
4. Inside the square, write the verb that means **control**.

regulate

Part 3

Write a word that comes from **digest** or **explain** in each blank. Fill in the correct circle for **noun, verb,** or **adjective**.

1. The book includes a few pages of _explanatory_ notes to help the reader understand the text.

   ○ noun   ○ verb   ● adjective

2. Do you have an _explanation_ as to why my lamp is broken?

   ● noun   ○ verb   ○ adjective

3. This liquid will help your _digestive_ problems.

   ○ noun   ○ verb   ● adjective

Definitions, following directions, context clues
Directions: If necessary, read the directions for each part. When students have completed the page, present each item and the answer. Correct any errors.

© 2001 SRA/McGraw-Hill. Permission is granted to reproduce for classroom use.   67

Part 5

Write the middle part of each deduction.

1. Snow falls when the temperature is low.
   Snow is falling in the mountains.
   So, the temperature in the mountains is low.

2. Citizens who vote are at least 18 years old.
   Maurice is a citizen who can vote.
   So, Maurice is at least 18 years old.

3. Some birds migrate south in the fall.
   Geese are birds.
   So, maybe geese migrate south in the fall.

Part 4

Read the story and answer the questions. Write **W** after each question that is answered by words in the story, and underline those words. Write **D** after each question that is answered by a deduction.

> The Jones Company manufactures automobiles. Almost everyone working for the Jones Company lives in the town of Thomasville. Some workers walk to the factory each morning because it is only a block or two from where they live. The Jones Company produces two different vehicles, the Jones Speedster and the Jones Minivan. The Jones Company makes sturdy cars.

1. What does the Jones Company manufacture? Automobiles (W)

2. Where is the Jones Company located? In or near Thomasville (D)

3. Why is the Jones Company's success important to Thomasville residents? Many of the residents work for the Jones Company. (D)

4. What two different vehicles does the Jones Company produce? The Jones Speedster and the Jones Minivan. (W)

☆ Part 6

Read each sentence. Decide whether it is a **statement**, a **question**, or an **exclamation**. Add the correct punctuation to each sentence.

1. Which team do you think will win ?
2. What a good player she is !
3. The ants got the cake !
4. I'm going to the library after school .
5. Where did you put my shoes ?
6. Let's run downstairs and hide !
7. Anna went fishing with her dad .
8. Did you say we should go inside ?

Identifying/evaluating deductions, types of sentences
Directions: If necessary, read the directions for each part. When students have completed the page, present each item and the answer. Correct any errors.

68   © 2001 SRA/McGraw-Hill. Permission is granted to reproduce for classroom use.

LESSON 35

Name _____

Part 1

Fill in each blank.
1. Spinal cord
2. Nerves
3. Brain

1 and 3. Central _____ nervous system
2. Peripheral _____ nervous system

Part 2

Write a word that comes from **participate** in each blank. Then fill in the circle for **noun, verb,** or **adjective.**

1. The teacher informed the class that each student would have to _participate_ in the class play.
   ○ noun ● verb ○ adjective

2. Jim will be _participating_ in the bazaar at his church on Saturday.
   ○ noun ● verb ○ adjective

3. Their _participation_ was crucial to the success of the business.
   ● noun ○ verb ○ adjective

4. She had a _participatory_ role in the musical.
   ○ noun ○ verb ● adjective

☆ Part 3

Read the following sentences. Decide whether each sentence is a question, a statement, or an exclamation. Fill in the circle next to the correct answer.

1. This a beautiful picture!
   ○ statement ○ question ● exclamation

2. My piano teacher said I was doing a good job.
   ● statement ○ question ○ exclamation

3. How many wishes did you make?
   ○ statement ● question ○ exclamation

LESSON 35

Name _____

Part 4

Fill in the circle beside the word that combines the sentences correctly. Combine the sentences with that word.

1. Kristen was always late for work.

   Kristen lost her job.

   ○ particularly ○ but ● because

   Kristen lost her job because she was always late for work.

2. The dog was barking loudly.

   The dog saw a squirrel.

   ○ but ○ particularly ● because

   The dog was barking loudly because it saw a squirrel.

3. The coffee shop brews coffee.

   The coffee shop fries doughnuts.

   ● and ○ particularly ○ because

   The coffee shop brews coffee and fries donuts.

4. Scott practices his multiplication facts every night.

   Scott never fails a math test.

   ● but ○ because ○ which

   Because Scott practices his multiplication facts every night, he never fails a math test.

Part 5

Underline the contradiction. Circle the statement it contradicts.

Bright blue liquid flowed through tubes in the lab. Some liquid was hotter than room temperature and some liquid was almost freezing. The lab looked like a jungle. The doctor said, "I know that all this liquid has the same amount of carbon dioxide. The reason is that all the liquid is now 56 degrees. If I get that carbon dioxide out of the liquid, I will sell it and make money."

LESSON 36

Name _____

Part 1

Tell **one** way that the things compared are **not** the same.

Tell **one** way that the things compared **are** the same.

> **Before the storm, the sky was like a bruise.**

1. (You cannot see the sky on your skin.)

2. (They are both black and blue.)

Part 2

Circle the subject and underline the predicate in each sentence. Rewrite each sentence by moving part of the predicate.

1. (Her grandma and her aunt) are coming to visit in a week.
   In a week, her grandma and her aunt are coming to visit.

2. (My mom) always goes jogging after work.
   After work, my mom always goes jogging.

3. (You) should always look both ways before crossing a street.
   Before crossing a street, you should always look both ways.

Part 3

For each sentence, write **two** sentences that have the underlined common part.

1. <u>Dan</u>, who is very athletic, runs a marathon every year.
   a. Dan runs a marathon every year.
   b. Dan is very athletic.

2. <u>Tiffany</u> got a raise and a bigger office.
   a. Tiffany got a raise.
   b. Tiffany got a bigger office.

3. <u>Rachel</u>, who is in sales, does a great deal of traveling for her job.
   a. Rachel does a great deal of traveling for her job.
   b. Rachel is in sales.

Figurative language/similes, conventions of grammar, writing sentences
Directions: If necessary, read the directions for each part. When students have completed the page, present each item and the answer. Correct any errors.

© 2001 SRA/McGraw-Hill. Permission is granted to reproduce for classroom use.

71

LESSON 36

Name _____

☆ Part 4

> An **adjective** is a word that describes a noun. It tells which one, how many, or what kind.
>
> The **blue** car   My **kind** brother
> Our **new** house   The **big** park

Read the sentences. Circle the adjective that describes the underlined noun.

1. (The) (gray) cat slept in (the) sun.
2. (The) (tiny) baby smiled at me.
3. (The) (big) icicle was hanging from (the) roof.
4. I am carrying (four) books.
5. (The) (sick) boy went home at lunch.
6. Can you find the (new) flag?
7. (The) (yellow) bird ate from (the) feeder.
8. (The) (apple) tree was by (the) garage.
9. Rose likes to eat (warm) cookies.
10. Teresa wants to open (two) presents.

Part 5

Fill in each blank with the word that has the same meaning as the word or words under the blank.

1. They wanted to __reside__ in a quiet
   (live somewhere)
   neighborhood.

2. Denise wanted to __examine__ the papers
   (look at)
   more thoroughly before signing them.

3. The students were asked to __select__
   (choose)
   a topic that they wanted to research.

4. The __conclusion__ of the movie was
   (end)
   not what she expected.

5. When he didn't understand the
   __explanation__, he asked his teacher
   (something that explains)
   to repeat it.

Adjectives, context clues
Directions: If necessary, read the directions for each part. When students have completed the page, present each item and the answer. Correct any errors.

72

© 2001 SRA/McGraw-Hill. Permission is granted to reproduce for classroom use.

168

☆ Part 1

Complete each sentence below with the best adjective from the box.

| blue | happy | secret | new | sandy |

1. The ___happy___ boy blew out all his candles.

2. Did the ___new___ car, you?

3. My sisters and I liked the ___blue___ clubhouse is hard car.

4. Our ___secret___ clubhouse is hard to find.

5. The ___sandy___ beach did not hurt my feet.

Part 2

Make up a simile for each item.

1. The kitten's legs were very skinny.
   (Her legs were like toothpicks.)

2. His hands were very soft.
   (His hands were like velvet.)

Part 3

Fill in each blank.

1. ___trachea___

2. ___bronchial tubes___

3. ___lungs___

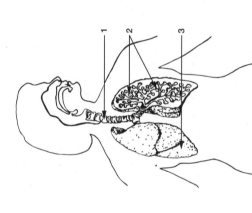

Adjectives, figurative language, graphic aids
Directions: If necessary, read the directions for each part. When students have completed the page, present each item and the answer. Correct any errors.

Part 4

For each sentence, write **two** sentences that have the underlined common part.

1. Heather and Carrie are riding bikes.
   a. Heather is riding a bike.

   b. Carrie is riding a bike.

2. You must follow the directions, which say to do only the odd-numbered questions.
   a. You must follow the directions.

   b. The directions say to do only the odd-numbered questions.

3. The movie was scary, but it was very good.
   a. The movie was scary.

   b. The movie was very good.

Part 5

Circle the subject and underline the predicate in each sentence.
Rewrite each sentence by moving part of the predicate.

1. (They) built a pool in their backyard.
   In their backyard, they built a pool.

2. (Terry and Rich) went to a baseball game in New York.
   In New York, Terry and Rich went to a baseball game.

3. (Driving) is not a good idea if you are tired.
   If you are tired, driving is not a good idea.

4. (Three thousand people) ran in a race last Monday.
   Last Monday, three thousand people ran in a race.

Writing sentences, conventions of grammar
Directions: If necessary, read the directions for each part. When students have completed the page, present each item and the answer. Correct any errors.

Part 1

Underline the contradiction. Circle the statement it contradicts. Tell **why** the underlined statement contradicts the circled statement. Make the underlined statement true.

> (Over time, some luxuries become needs.) The first people on Earth didn't need much to live; raw meat, water, and a cave. Later, somebody discovered fire, and people started using it. They didn't really need fire, but they liked it. Now they could cook their food and warm their caves at night. Over time they got so used to cooking food and keeping warm that they couldn't live without fire. <u>Fire had started out as a need and become a luxury.</u> The same thing happened with shoes, cups, plates, chairs, beds, and many other things.

Some luxuries become needs, not the other way around.

Part 2

Write the instructions.

```
        ①
trachea ③
        ②
```

1. (what) (Draw a horizontal line.)

2. (what and where) (Draw a second horizontal line below the first line.)

3. (what and where) (Write the word trachea between the two lines.)

☆ Part 3

Read the sentences. Circle the adjectives used in each sentence.

1. (My) (favorite) food is (fried) chicken.
2. (Our) (old) car wouldn't start on such a (cold) morning.
3. (The) (old) dog limped down (the) (long) street.
4. (The) (tired) hiker tripped on (the) (big) rock.
5. A (furry) rabbit crossed (the) (narrow) path.
6. (The) (two) skaters glided on (the) (smooth) ice.
7. (Her) (long) hair was tied in (two) braids.
8. (The) (little) boy ate (the) (last) apple.

Part 4

Tell whether each action is controlled by a **sense** nerve or a **motor** nerve. Fill in the correct circle.

1. "Open the window."   ○ sense   ● motor
2. "Smell cake."   ● sense   ○ motor
3. "Touch the cake."   ○ sense   ● motor
4. "Hear music."   ● sense   ○ motor
5. "Answer the phone."   ○ sense   ● motor
6. "Stomach hurts."   ● sense   ○ motor

Part 5

Fill in the circle beside the word that combines the sentences correctly. Combine the sentences with that word.

1. Today, the sun is shining.
Today, rain is falling.
● but   ○ particularly   ○ who
Today, the sun is shining, but rain is falling.

2. Baseball is considered America's pastime.
Abner Doubleday invented baseball.
○ because   ○ but   ● which
Abner Doubleday invented baseball, which is considered America's pastime.

3. I like candy.
I like fruit-flavored candy the most.
● particularly   ○ which   ○ because
I like candy, particularly fruit-flavored candy.

4. John was bored.
John fell asleep while watching the race.
● because   ○ which   ○ but
John fell asleep while watching the race because he was bored.

5. San Marino is located in Europe.
San Marino is an extremely small country.
○ but   ○ particularly   ● which
San Marino, which is an extremely small country, is located in Europe.

6. Carlos passed the test.
Carlos won a prize at the science fair.
● and   ○ but   ○ which
Carlos passed the test and won a prize at the science fair.

170

LESSON 39

Name _____

Part 1

For each word on the left, write the letter of its definition on the right.

1. consumable   e   a. (v.) say that something will happen
2. participation   c   b. (v.) build
3. supply   f   c. (n.) the act of participating
4. predict   a   d. (v.) make in a factory
5. demand   h   e. (a.) that something can be consumed
6. obtain   g   f. (n.) how much there is of something
7. construct   b   g. (v.) get
8. manufacture   d   h. (n.) how well something sells

☆ Part 2

An **adverb** describes a verb. It may answer the question *how, how often, when,* or *where.*

Read the sentences. Circle the adverb or adverbs used in each sentence, and tell whether each adverb answers the question **how, how often, when** or **where.** The first one is done for you.

1. We (finally) arrived at the hotel.   **When**
2. He (quickly) finished his homework.
   How
3. My cat ran (away).   **Where**
4. The band played (loudly).   **How**
5. Don't run (near) the river.   **Where**
6. I get up (early) in the morning.   **When**

Part 3

Write a word that comes from **participate** or **manufacture** in each blank. Fill in the correct circle for **noun, verb,** or **adjective.**

1. Yesterday, I __participated__ in a soccer match against my cousin's team.
  ◯ **noun**   ⬤ **verb**   ◯ **adjective**

2. Tyrone is a __manufacturer__ of solid wood furniture.
  ⬤ **noun**   ◯ **verb**   ◯ **adjective**

3. __Participation__ in the new club has been less than we had hoped.
  ⬤ **noun**   ◯ **verb**   ◯ **adjective**

4. Chan __participated__ in many different clubs at school last year.
  ◯ **noun**   ⬤ **verb**   ◯ **adjective**

LESSON 39

Name _____

Part 4

Underline the common part. For each sentence, write **two** sentences with that common part.

1. Manny, who is from Colombia, likes to watch television.
 a. __Manny likes to watch television.__
 b. __Manny is from Colombia.__

2. Sheila joined the choir at her school because she likes to sing.
 a. __Sheila joined the choir at her school.__
 b. __Sheila likes to sing.__

3. The boat crashed into a hidden rock, but it did not sink.
 a. __The boat crashed into a hidden rock.__
 b. __The boat did not sink.__

Part 5

Use the facts to fill out the form.

> **Facts: You are auditioning for the role of a television superhero. All your life, you have dreamed of being a superhero. You have been acting in plays for ten years. The director of the television show once hired your wife to appear in a commercial. You are twenty-six years old. Your name is Damon Stevens. Your address is 449 Liverpool Avenue, Fremont, California.**

Instructions:
 a. Print your address on line 1.
 b. Write what you are auditioning for on line 7.
 c. On line 3, state what you have always dreamed of being.
 d. State your age on line 5.
 e. On line 2, tell how many years of acting experience you have.
 f. Write your full name on line 4.

1. __449 Liverpool Avenue__
 __Fremont, California__
2. __Ten years__
3. __A superhero__
4. __Damon Stevens__
5. __Twenty-six__
6. __A role as a superhero__

Name _____

Part 1

Underline the redundant sentences.

> After a long day working in his fields, Farmer John is ready to take a nap. When he arrives at his house, he cooks himself some dinner. He is very tired from working so hard in his fields. John has two sisters, Edna and Martha, who like to help him work in his fields and feed his horses. Edna lives in a blue house next to John's farm, and Martha lives in a small house in town. Martha's house is very small. Her favorite part of the day is when she goes out to John's farm to ride her horse, Majestic. Edna enjoys plowing John's cornfields, particularly the field between the river and the forest. Edna likes to look at the river and the trees while she works in the fields.

☆ Part 2

Finish each sentence by choosing an **adverb** from the word box and writing it in the blank.

| somewhere | Yesterday | perfectly | carefully |

1. __Yesterday__ Dad and I went grocery shopping.

2. Tom lost his coat __somewhere__ near the school.

3. The art teacher __carefully__ cut the tissue paper with her scissors.

4. Margaret skated __perfectly__. She made no mistakes.

Conventions of grammar/revising, adverbs, identifying facts
Directions: If necessary, read the directions for each part. When students have competed the page, present each item and the answer. Correct any errors.

© 2001 SRA/McGraw-Hill. Permission is granted to reproduce for classroom use.

Part 3

Read the story and answer the questions.
Write **W** after each question that is answered by words in the story, and underline those words.
Write **D** after each question that is answered by a deduction.

> **David tried to be a smart shopper.** Good shoppers get more and spend less. Before he went shopping, David read a consumer report about buying food. When he went shopping, David looked for the best deals. He bought grade B eggs because they were cheaper than grade A eggs but just as good. He acquired a big bag of flour because the big bag cost less per pound. David paid a lot of money for the food he bought, but he would have paid a lot more if he hadn't been such a smart shopper.

1. Was David a smart shopper? __Yes (D)__

2. Why did David buy grade B eggs? __They were cheaper than Grade A eggs, but just as good. (W)__

3. Green bananas cost $.29 per pound. Ripe bananas cost $.39 per pound. Which kind of bananas did David buy? __Green (D)__

Name _____

Part 4

Rewrite the paragraph in four sentences on the lines below. If one of the sentences tells **why,** combine the sentences with **because.** If the sentences seem contradictory, combine them with **but.**

> Monroe and Sharon like horses. Monroe and Sharon like quarter horses the most. They own eight horses. They do not like all of them. Monroe has been training his horse for months. Monroe will compete in a contest on Saturday. The contest will take place in Columbus. Columbus is the capital of Ohio.

Monroe and Sharon like horses, particularly quarter horses. They own eight horses, but they do not like all of them. Monroe has been training his horse for months because he will compete in a contest on Saturday. The contest will take place in Columbus, which is the capital of Ohio.

Part 5

1. What's the rule about when the supply is greater than the demand?
When the supply is greater than the demand, the price goes down.

> **In the summer, the supply of snow shovels is greater than the demand for snow shovels.**

2. What will happen to the price of shovels?
The price will go down.

3. How do you know?
The supply is greater than the demand.

> **Due to last year's flood, the demand for corn is greater than the supply of corn.**

4. What will happen to the price of corn?
The price will go up.

5. How do you know?
The demand is greater than the supply.

Conventions of grammar/writing, drawing conclusions based on evidence
Directions: If necessary, read the directions for each part. When students have completed the page, present each item and the answer. Correct any errors.

80

© 2001 SRA/McGraw-Hill. Permission is granted to reproduce for classroom use.

172

Part 1

Write a word that comes from **manufacture** or **participate** in each blank. Fill in the circle for **noun, verb,** or **adjective.**

1. Class __participation__ is required in order to earn an "A."

   ● noun   ○ verb   ○ adjective

2. America and Japan __manufacture__ thousands of cars each week.

   ○ noun   ● verb   ○ adjective

3. It is important for airplane __manufacturers__ to follow certain rules and regulations.

   ● noun   ○ verb   ○ adjective

4. If people work for a bike __manufacturing__ plant, they make bikes.

   ○ noun   ○ verb   ● adjective

5. All fourth graders will __participate__ in the science fair this spring.

   ○ noun   ● verb   ○ adjective

Part 2

Underline the contradiction. Circle the statement it contradicts. Tell **why** the underlined statement contradicts the circled statement. Make the underlined statement true.

Corn farmers have to protect their crops from many different bugs. Many times in the past, bugs have wiped out corn crops. Last year, bugs ate a lot of corn, and there was not enough corn for everybody who wanted it. (The price of corn was very) high. The farmers tried everything to get rid of the bugs. They sprayed powder from planes. They tried to find animals that would eat the bugs. Because there was so little corn, the price of corn continued to drop. One company started manufacturing seeds that were bugproof. All in all, it was a very bad year for farmers.

When the demand is greater than the supply, prices go up.

Part 3

Follow the directions.

1. Draw a rectangle.

2. Draw a vertical line through the middle of the rectangle.

3. Draw a horizontal line through the middle of the vertical line.

4. In the bottom left part of the rectangle, write the word that means **make in a factory.**

manufacture	

Inflectional and derivational suffixes, contradictions, following directions
Directions: If necessary, read the directions for each part. When students have completed the page, present each item and the answer. Correct any errors.

© 2001 SRA/McGraw-Hill. Permission is granted to reproduce for classroom use.

81

☆ Part 4

Complete each sentence with an **adverb** from the box below. Choose an adverb that answers the question in ( ). Answers may vary.

far	early	quickly
	near	late	slowly

1. Jim walked __slowly__. (How?)

2. I got home __early__ from cheerleading practice. (When?)

3. The fire was __near__ the center of town. (Where?)

4. Sheila ran __quickly__ to her bike. (How?)

5. It was __late__ by the time we ate dinner. (When?)

6. We live __far__ from the school. (Where?)

Part 5

Tell **two** ways that the things compared **are** the same. Tell **one** way that they are **not** the same.

Her teeth were like snow.

1. (They are both white.)

2. (They both sparkle.)

3. (Her teeth are not soft like snow.)

Part 6

Write the conclusion of each deduction.

1. Some doctors perform surgery.

   David is a doctor.

   So, maybe David performs surgery.

2. Vegetables grow in gardens.

   A carrot is a vegetable.

   So, carrots grow in gardens.

3. Mammals are animals that have hair.

   Dogs have hair.

   So, dogs are mammals.

Adverbs, figurative language, drawing conclusions
Directions: If necessary, read the directions for each part. When students have completed the page, present each item and the answer. Correct any errors.

82

© 2001 SRA/McGraw-Hill. Permission is granted to reproduce for classroom use.

Part 1

Underline the redundant sentences.

Last summer, everybody in Centerville wanted a pair of sandals. Mr. Jones ran the only shoe store in town. There was a big demand for sandals. Mr. Jones got lots of sandals from a manufacturer. No other place in town sold sandals. Mr. Jones made one dollar on each pair of sandals that he sold. One day, Mr. Jones sold ninety pairs of sandals. He made ninety dollars from sandal sales that day.

☆ Part 2

Facts are details that can be proven true. Opinions are what someone thinks. They can't be proven true. Read each sentence below. Write **F** for fact or **O** for opinion.

F ___ 1. Whales live in the ocean.

O ___ 2. Playing tennis is a fun sport.

F ___ 3. Carrots grow in the ground.

F ___ 4. Sacramento is the capital of California.

F ___ 5. Green beans are good for you.

O ___ 6. Fifth grade is the best grade.

83

Part 3

For each sentence, write **two** sentences with that common part.

1. Jeremy and Carrie have many toys.

a. Jeremy has many toys.

b. Carrie has many toys.

2. That park, which is on the other side of town, has a lot of trees.

a. That park has a lot of trees!

b. That park is on the other side of town.

3. Patrick fixed his car, which needed new brakes.

a. Patrick fixed his car.

b. His car needed new brakes.

4. The puppy, which was abandoned by his owner, was hungry and cold.

a. The puppy was abandoned by his owner.

b. The puppy was hungry and cold.

Part 4

Combine the sentences with **although**.

1. Fred was not a fast runner.

Fred won the race.

Although Fred was not a fast runner, he won the race.

2. The team lost the championship.

The players were happy the team had a good season.

Although the team lost the championship, the players were happy they had a good season.

3. Susan was tired from a busy weekend.

Susan went to the grocery store Sunday night.

Although Susan was tired from a busy weekend, she went to the grocery store Sunday night.

Part 5

Follow the directions.

1. Draw a big circle.

2. Draw a horizontal line from the left side of the circle to the right side of the circle.

3. Draw a vertical line from the top of the circle to the bottom of the circle.

4. In the top right part of the circle, write the word that means **use up** or **eat**.

Part 6

Write the middle part of each deduction.

1. Feelings travel on sense nerves.

Pain is a feeling.

So, pain travels on sense nerves.

2. Commands travel on motor nerves.

"Move arm" is a command.

So, "Move arm" travels on motor nerves.

3. Some diseases damage nerves.

Polio is a disease.

So, maybe polio damages nerves.

Part 1

Fill in each blank with the word that has the same meaning as the word or words under the blank.

1. The ___conclusion___ of the play
   (end)
   surprised the audience.

2. He ___selected___ a video the whole
   (chose)
   family could enjoy.

3. Mr. Warga ___criticized___ the student
   (found fault with)
   for talking in the assembly.

4. Please ___explain___ the solution to
   (make things easier to understand)
   the math problem to the class.

Part 2

Combine the sentences with **although.**

1. Elizabeth exercised every day.
   Elizabeth did not get any thinner.
   Although Elizabeth exercised every
   day, she did not get any thinner.

2. Cody was sick.
   Cody could eat his dinner.
   Although Cody was sick, he could
   eat his dinner.

3. Terry finished his homework.
   Terry did not understand his math.
   Although Terry finished his
   homework, he did not understand
   his math.

4. Marcia was sleepy.
   Marcia finished the book.
   Although Marcia was sleepy, she
   finished the book.

Part 3

Cross out the wrong word and write the correct word above it. (4)

> My dog is a bulldog. Many people ~~is~~ are
> afraid of bulldogs, but my dog is a very
>   go
> nice dog. We ~~goes~~ walking every day in
> the park. At home, I keep him tied in the
>   gets
> backyard, but sometimes he ~~get~~ loose. If
> you ever see a bulldog with a green
>   His
> collar, that's my dog. ~~Her~~ name is Sam.

☆ Part 4

Read each sentence below. Underline it if it gives a fact. Circle it if it gives an opinion.

1. (Pigs do not smell good.)
2. There are four seasons in a year.
3. (I love homemade soup!)
4. There are seven continents.
5. (March is the best month of the year.)
6. (Basketball is the best sport.)
7. When hot air rises, it cools off.
8. Thanksgiving is in November.

Part 5

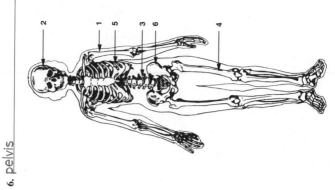

Fill in each blank.

1. __humerus__
2. __skull__
3. __spine__
4. __femur__
5. __ribs__
6. __pelvis__

Part 1

Make up a simile for each item.

1. Her eyes are blue.
   (Her eyes are like the ocean.)

2. He is so busy.
   (He is as busy as a bee.)

Part 2

Write the instructions.

③ productive   production
    ①   ②

1. (Draw a line that slants up to the left.)

2. (Write the word production to the right of the line.)

3. (Write the word productive to the left of the line.)

Part 3

Use the facts to fill out the form.

> **Facts: Your name is Julia Wilson. You have just graduated from State University in Laurelville. Your field is elementary education. You are applying for a teaching job at the local elementary school. You are twenty-two years old. You are newly married and unemployed. Your address is 657 North Broad, Wilmington, North Carolina. You want to teach fourth grade.**

Instructions:

1. Name, last name first (please print):
   Wilson, Julia

2. Colleges or universities attended:
   State University

3. What is your field?
   Elementary education

4. Current employer:
   None

5. Address? 657 North Broad
   Wilmington, North Carolina

6. What grade do you prefer to teach?
   Fourth

Figurative language/similes, writing instructions, identifying facts
Directions: If necessary, read the directions for each part. When students have completed the page, present each item and the answer. Correct any errors.

© 2001 SRA/McGraw-Hill. Permission is granted to reproduce for classroom use.

Part 4

For each word on the left, write the letter of its definition on the right.

1. participate — d
2. circulate — e
3. respiratory — i
4. oxygen — g
5. carbon dioxide — c
6. redundant — h
7. explanation — a
8. respire — b
9. criticize — f
10. digestive — j

a. (*n.*) something that explains
b. (*v.*) breathe
c. (*n.*) a gas that burning things produce
d. (*v.*) take part in something
e. (*v.*) move around
f. (*v.*) find fault with
g. (*n.*) a gas that burning things need
h. (*a.*) that something repeats what has already been said
i. (*a.*) that something involves respiration
j. (*a.*) that something involves digestion

☆ Part 5

Read the following paragraph. Draw a line under each sentence that tells a fact. Circle each sentences that give opinions.

> (Cooking is a lot of fun.) Some people are chefs. Their job is to cook. Many chefs go to cooking school. Both men and women can be chefs. (Home cooking is better than a chef's cooking.) Hotels, restaurants, schools and even airlines have chefs. (It would be a fun job to be a chef.)

Part 6

Write the middle part of each deduction.

1. Some blood vessels go to the heart.
   <u>Venules are blood vessels.</u>
   So, maybe venules go to the heart.

2. Blood that is almost black carries carbon dioxide.
   <u>Blood in the vena cava is almost black.</u>
   So, blood in the vena cava carries carbon dioxide.

Vocabulary, fact and opinion, deductions
Directions: If necessary, read the directions for each part. When students have completed the page, present each item and the answer. Correct any errors.

88   © 2001 SRA/McGraw-Hill. Permission is granted to reproduce for classroom use.

176

LESSON 45   Name

Part 1

Underline the common part. For each sentence, write two sentences with that common part.

1. This man and that woman want to reside in town.

   a. This man wants to reside in town.

   b. That woman wants to reside in town.

2. He likes his residence because it is old.

   a. He likes his residence.

   b. His residence is old.

Part 2

meat   leather

1. Tell how the objects could be alike.
   (They are both tough.)

2. Write a simile about the objects.
   (That meat was like leather.)

Part 3

1. What is the rule about when the demand is less than the supply?
   When the demand is less than the supply, prices go down.

2. What is the rule about what manufacturers try to do?
   Manufacturers try to make the demand greater than the supply.

3. What is the rule about when the demand is greater than the supply?
   When the demand is greater than the supply, prices go up.

Part 4

Circle the subject and underline the predicate in each sentence. Rewrite each sentence by moving part of the predicate.

1. (Everyone) was cold last winter.
   Last winter, everyone was cold.

2. (Many people) walk quickly in New York.
   In New York, many people walk quickly.

Conventions of grammar, comparisons/figurative language, writing
Directions: Read the directions to each item with the student. Give the student time to respond before going to the next item. When the student has completed the page, go over the items and answers. Correct any errors.

LESSON 45   Name

Part 5

Fill in the circle next to the word that combines the sentences correctly. Combine the sentences with that word.

1. Hector acquired a car.

   Hector still rides his bike.

   ○ which   ○ because   ● but

   Hector acquired a car, but he still rides his bike.

2. Tom was going to the party.

   His friend was going to the party.

   ○ who   ○ particularly   ● and

   Tom and his friend were going to the party.

3. That book was predictable.

   That book was most predictable near the end.

   ● particularly   ○ because   ○ however

   That book was predictable, particularly near the end.

★ Part 6

• A prefix comes before a base word. Here are some examples of words with prefixes.
   untied   redraw   disobey
• The prefixes **un-** and **dis-** mean "not."
   The prefix **re-** means "again."

Read the word in front of each sentence. Add a prefix to that word and write it in the sentence.

1. **heat** Should I _reheat_ the soup?

2. **fair** It is _unfair_ that we can't go to the movie.

3. **agree** It is all right to _disagree_ when you have a good reason.

4. **paint** Marcia wants to _repaint_ her house.

5. **connect** If you _disconnect_ the computer, it won't run.

6. **sure** Susan was _unsure_ of the phone number.

Writing/conventions of grammar, prefixes
Directions: If necessary, read the directions for each part. When students have completed the page, present each item and the answer. Correct any errors.

Name _____

Part 1

Answer the questions.

1. What's the rule about when the demand is greater than the supply?

When the demand is greater than the supply, prices go up.

In the fall, the demand for warm coats is greater than the supply of warm coats.

2. What will happen to the price of warm coats?

It will go up.

3. How do you know?

The demand is greater than the supply.

Last year, the price of gasoline went up.

4. Which was greater, the supply or the demand?

The demand was greater.

5. How do you know?

The price went up.

Part 2

hair   weeds

1. Tell how the objects could be alike.

They both grow fast.

2. Write a simile about the objects.

His hair grew like weeds.

Part 3

Cross out the wrong word and write the correct word above it. (4)

Last year, Tom had two hamsters. He
kept ~~it~~ them in a cage. One night, the hamsters
got out of the cage. ~~It~~ They ran under the bed
and wouldn't come out. Tom had to
crawl under the bed to grab ~~her~~ his hamsters.
He pulled them out by their tails and
put ~~it~~ them back in the cage.

Name _____

☆ Part 4

Underline each word that begins with a prefix.

1. pack, <u>repack</u>
2. copy, <u>recopy</u>
3. <u>unsure</u>, sure
4. <u>relive</u>, live
5. tie, <u>untie</u>
6. <u>rename</u>, name
7. make, <u>remake</u>
8. <u>untrue</u>, true
9. connect, <u>disconnect</u>
10. <u>disappear</u>, appear

Part 5

Underline the common part. For each sentence, write **two** sentences with that common part.

1. People get cold particularly in the winter.
   a. People get cold.

   b. People get cold in the winter.

2. Her mother and father are talking about money.
   a. Her mother is talking about money.

   b. Her father is talking about money.

3. The doctor checked the man's respiration, which was loud.
   a. The doctor checked the man's respiration.

   b. The man's respiration was loud.

4. The demand for gas, which is great, increases each year.
   a. The demand for gas increases each year.

   b. The demand for gas is great.

LESSON 47   Name

Part 1

Rewrite the story in six sentences on the lines below.

German shepherd dogs were first used to protect herds of sheep, which were often attacked by wolves. German shepherds were used by the police, who trained them to sniff out criminals. Today, German shepherds are used as watchdogs and as guide dogs for the blind.

German shepherd dogs were
first used to protect herds of
sheep. Herds of sheep were
often attacked by wolves.
German shepherds were used
by the police. The police
trained them to sniff out
criminals. Today, German
shepherds are used as
watchdogs. Today, German
shepherds are used as guide
dogs for the blind.

Part 2

hands   ice

1. Tell how the objects could be alike.
   (They could both be cold.)

2. Write a simile about the objects.
   (His hands were like ice.)

Part 3

Fill in each blank with the word or words under the blank.

1. Storms ___erode___ the beach.
   (wear down)

2. Did the company ever ___manufacture___
   (make in a factory)
   paper?

3. Ted saw the dog ___consume___ his food.
   (eat)

4. Please do not ___criticize___ your sister.
   (find fault with)

5. Your ___respiration___ increases after
   (the act of respiring)
   heavy activity.

LESSON 47   Name

Part 4

Underline the redundant sentences.

Some people read magazines. ~~Some people don't.~~ The store had many different kinds of magazines. John wanted to acquire a magazine, so he went to the store. The store had a wide selection of magazines. John looked for a magazine about cars. ~~The store had ten different car magazines.~~ John couldn't decide which one to buy. ~~The store had more than one car magazine.~~ John didn't know which one he wanted.

☆ Part 5

Complete each sentence by adding **un-**, **dis-**, or **re-** to the word in parentheses.

1. The man looked ___unconcerned___ about
   (concerned)
   what would happen to him.

2. My teacher asked me to ___redo___ the
   (do)
   paper.

3. Terry said that he ___dislikes___ brussel
   (likes)
   sprouts.

Part 6

Follow the directions.

1. Draw a horizontal line.

2. Draw another horizontal line below the first line.

3. Draw a line that slants from the right end of the top line to the left end of the bottom line.

4. On the lower horizontal line, write the word that means **find fault with**.

criticize

Part 1

Rewrite the story in six sentences on the lines below.

> Diamonds and coal are made of the same mineral, which is carbon. Diamonds are used for jewelry and in industry. Colored diamonds are hard to find because they are quite rare.

Diamonds and coal are made

of the same mineral. The

mineral is carbon. Diamonds are

used for jewelry. Diamonds are

used in industry. Colored

diamonds are hard to find.

Colored diamonds are quite

rare.

_____

Part 2

Write a word that comes from **reside** or **conclude** in each blank. Fill in the circle for **verb, noun,** or **adjective.**

1. The people clapped when Bob __concluded__ his speech.
   ● verb   ○ noun   ○ adjective

2. Many snakes __reside__ in warm places.
   ● verb   ○ noun   ○ adjective

3. The __conclusion__ of the story was sad.
   ○ verb   ● noun   ○ adjective

4. Some __residential__ areas are for older people.
   ○ verb   ● noun   ○ adjective

5. Jim __concluded__ that the power was off.
   ● verb   ○ noun   ○ adjective

Writing, inflectional and derivational suffixes
Directions: If necessary, read the directions for each part. When students have completed the page, present each item and answer. Correct any errors.
© 2001 SRA/McGraw-Hill. Permission is granted to reproduce for classroom use.

Part 3

Tell if each nerve is a **sense** nerve or a **motor** nerve. Draw an arrow to show which way each message moves.

1. "Curl toes."
2. "Food smells good."

sense

motor

sense

motor

2. "Lie down."
4. "Feel tired."

Part 4

town   beehive

1. Tell how the objects could be alike.
   (They are both busy.)

2. Write a simile about the objects.
   (The town was like a beehive.)

☆ Part 5

> • A **suffix** is added at the end of a word and changes the meaning of the word or the way the word is used in a sentence.
>
> thankful   careless   teacher
>
> The suffix -**ful** means "full of."
> The suffix -**less** means "without."
> The suffix -**er** means "one who does."

Read the base word below. Add the suffix and write the new word.

1. age + less = __ageless__
2. paint + er = __painter__
3. tire + less = __tireless__
4. joy + ful = __joyful__
5. fear + ful = __fearful__

Graphic aids, figurative language, suffixes
Directions: If necessary, read the directions for each part. When students have completed the page, present each item and answer. Correct any errors.
© 2001 SRA/McGraw-Hill. Permission is granted to reproduce for classroom use.

LESSON 49

Name _____

Part 1

Combine the sentences with **although**.

1. Steven interviewed for the job.

   Steven didn't get the job.

   Although Steven interviewed
   for the job, he didn't get it.

2. She didn't have all the facts.

   Her conclusions were correct.

   Although she didn't have all the
   facts, her conclusions were correct.

3. Jessica enjoyed cats more than dogs.

   Jessica had a dog for a pet.

   Although Jessica enjoyed cats more
   than dogs, she had a dog for a pet.

4. Carl's sink was broken.

   Carl didn't call the plumber for two weeks.

   Although Carl's sink was broken, he
   didn't call a plumber for two weeks.

5. It rained the morning of the party.

   It turned out to be a beautiful day.

   Although it rained the morning of
   the party, it turned out to be a
   beautiful day.

Part 2

Read the story and answer the questions.

> Mr. Jones runs the only dairy farm near Mudville. In January, his cows produce just as much milk as Mudville needs. Mr. Jones makes $1,000 from milk sales that month. In February, his cows produce a lot less milk than Mudville needs. If Mr. Jones sells the milk at the old price, he won't make $1,000 because he doesn't have as much milk to sell. But Mr. Jones wants to make $1,000, so he raises his price. Mudville's demand for milk is much greater than Mr. Jones's supply, and he has no trouble selling his milk at the higher price.

1. What's the rule about demand and supply?
   When the demand is greater
   than the supply, prices go up.

2. If Mr. Jones sells his milk at the old price, why won't he make $1,000?
   It is because he doesn't have as
   much milk to sell.

3. Why did he raise his prices? It is
   because he wants to make $1,000.

Conventions of grammar/writing sentences, identifying facts
Directions: If necessary, read the directions for each part. When students have completed the page, present each item and the answer. Correct any errors.

97

LESSON 49

Name _____

Part 3

For each word on the left, write the letter of its definition on the right.

1. circulate	_f_	a. (n.) the body system of nerves
2. nervous system	_a_	b. (n.) something that protects
3. conclude	_h_	c. (n.) something that is selected
4. protection	_b_	d. (v.) breathe
5. residence	_e_	e. (n.) a place where someone resides
6. respire	_d_	f. (v.) move around
7. selection	_c_	g. (n.) a statement that tells how things are the same
8. simile	_g_	h. (v.) end or figure out

Part 4

Write the conclusion of each deduction.

1. Every human heart has four chambers.

   Joe is human.

   So, Joe's heart has four
   chambers.

2. Some plants produce resin.

   Trees are plants.

   So, maybe trees produce
   resin.

3. All nerves carry messages.

   The vagus is a nerve.

   So, the vagus carries
   messages.

☆ Part 5

Add one of the **suffixes** from the box below to each underlined word to fit the meaning. Write the new word that is formed.

> -ful   -ness   -er

1. Someone who helps a lot is ___helpful___.

2. A person who teaches is a ___teacher___.

3. The state of being happy is ___happiness___.

4. Someone who paints is a ___painter___.

5. The state of being dark is ___darkness___.

6. Someone who likes to play is ___playful___.

Definitions, deductions, suffixes
Directions: If necessary, read the directions for each part. When students have completed the page, present each item and answer. Correct any errors.

98

LESSON 50   Name _____

Part 1

Fill in the circle beside the word that combines the sentences correctly. Combine the sentences with that word.

1. That con man has sold many phony tickets.

His pal has sold many phony tickets.

○ however   ● and   ○ which

That con man and his pal have

sold many phony tickets.

2. The man took medicine.

The man was sick.

○ but   ○ which   ● because

The man took medicine

because he was sick.

3. Minnesota has many lakes.

Minnesota is in the north.

● which   ○ but   ○ because

Minnesota, which is in the

north, has many lakes.

Part 2

Underline the contradiction. Circle the statement it contradicts. Tell **why** the underlined statement contradicts the circled statement. Make the underlined statement true.

When Mel finished high school, he left Columbus for a year. While he was away, construction workers modified every building on Main Street. Many people moved into the city, and the city had to make new regulations. Most people predicted that Columbus would keep growing. When Mel came back, he hardly recognized the city. All kinds of new people were walking on the sidewalks. His friends were saying that Columbus would get bigger. As he walked down Main Street, he noticed that the barber shop was still the same.

If every building on Main

Street was modified, the

barber shop could not still

be the same.

LESSON 50   Name _____

Part 3

Write **P** if the underlined word has a prefix. Write **S** if it has a suffix. Write **P** and **S** if the word has both.

1. __S__ It is doubtful that anyone will understand.

2. __S__ The painter wanted to move out west.

3. __P__ They could not undo what they had done.

4. __PS__ The thieves disappeared.

5. __S__ She was full of goodness.

6. __P__ The teacher said to recopy the letter.

7. __PS__ The magazine was discontinued.

8. __S__ I was fearful of diving off the board.

Part 4

Cross out the wrong word and write the correct word above it.

Louis Armstrong ~~camed~~ to Chicago in the
                    came

1920s. He started ~~her~~ own band. He began to
                   his

make recordings. Louis Armstrong's recordings

~~was~~ probably the most important recordings
were

ever made. His recordings inspired jazz

musicians all over the country. Soon, many jazz

bands ~~was~~ formed in Chicago and New York.
       were

Part 5

Write the instructions.

1. Draw a horizontal line.

2. From the right end of the horizontal line, draw a longer line that slants up and to the left.

3. Connect the ends of the two lines.

LESSON 51

Name _____

Part 1

skin   milk

1. Tell how the objects could be alike.
   (They could both be white.)

2. Write a simile about the objects.
   (He skin was like milk.)

Part 2

Use the facts to fill out the form.

> **Facts: Your name is Jake Howard. You have lived at 1255 Lake Avenue for two years. Your rent is $400 a month, and your car payments are $250 a month. You were born on October 11, 1973. Your first job, which you started in 1992, was with the American Title Company. Since 1994, you have worked for Juniper Credit, and you make $2,000 a month. You have one credit card, and you are newly married. You are filling out a credit application to buy a washer and dryer.**

Instructions:

1. Name, last name first: Howard, Jake

2. Age: (This year minus 1973)

3. Most recent employer:
   Juniper Credit

4. Monthly income: $2,000.00

5. Total monthly rent and car payments:
   $650.00

Part 3

Rewrite the story in four sentences on the lines below. If one of the sentences tells **why**, combine the sentences with **because**. If two sentences seem contradictory, combine them with **but**.

> Finally, Magellan came to an island called Cebu. Cebu is in the southern Philippine Islands. Magellan thought that his trip was almost over. Magellan was still very far from home. Magellan died on Cebu. Magellan got into a fight. His crew fled Cebu. His crew kept on sailing.

Finally, Magellan came to an island called Cebu, which is in the southern Philippine Islands. Magellan thought that his trip was almost over, but he was still very far from home. Magellan died on Cebu because he got into a fight. His crew fled Cebu and kept on sailing.

Figurative language, identifying facts, writing, conventions of grammar
Directions: If necessary, read the directions for each part. When students have completed the page, present each item and the answer. Correct any errors.

LESSON 51

Name _____

Part 4

Write a word that comes from **predict** or **digest** in each blank. Then fill in the circle for **verb**, **noun**, or **adjective**.

1. Andy is _predicting_ the winner of the game.
   ● verb   ○ noun   ○ adjective

2. Her _digestive_ system includes her esophagus and her liver.
   ○ verb   ○ noun   ● adjective

3. She ate peppermint to help her _digestion_.
   ○ verb   ● noun   ○ adjective

4. Things that are _predictable_ are often dull.
   ○ verb   ○ noun   ● adjective

5. The fortune-teller loved to make _predictions_.
   ○ verb   ● noun   ○ adjective

6. _Digesting_ some food can be hard on your stomach.
   ● verb   ○ noun   ○ adjective

☆ Part 5

> The first word of a sentence is capitalized.
> **T**he wind took my kite into the sky.
>
> The word *I* is always written with a capital letter.
> Cory and **I** are going to the play.
>
> Names of people and places begin with a capital letter.
> **D**r. **M**eek **A**lbany, **N**ew **Y**ork
> **F**ranklin **S**treet **C**anada
>
> Days of the week and months of the year are capitalized.
> **M**onday, **M**ay 6; **T**uesday, **W**ednesday

Rewrite the words that should be capitalized.

1. ridge road   Ridge Road
2. denver, colorado   Denver, Colorado
3. dr. ortiz   Dr. Ortiz
4. north america   North America
5. second street   Second Street
6. friday   Friday
7. mexico   Mexico
8. mr. Carver   Mr. Carver
9. princeton road   Princeton Road
10. rumson, new jersey Rumson, New Jerse

Inflectional and derivational suffixes, capitalization
Directions: If necessary, read the directions for each part. When students have completed the page, present each item and the answer. Correct any errors.

Part 1

Answer the questions.

1. What's the rule about products that are readier to use?

   Products that are readier to

   use cost more.

2. Which is readier to use, a cake or a cake mix?

   A cake.

3. So, what else do you know about a cake?

   It costs more.

4. How do you know?

   It is readier to use.

5. Which costs more, a bike that's put together or a bike that comes in parts?

   A bike that's put together

6. How do you know?

   It is readier to use.

Mr. Thompson gets cooked pork in a restaurant.
Mr. Rodriguez gets raw pork in a store and then spends an hour cooking it.

7. Whose pork costs more?

   Mr. Thompson's

8. How do you know?

   It is readier to use.

Part 2

Underline the nouns. Draw a line **over** the adjectives. Circle the verbs.

1. Burning things (need) oxygen.

2. That thermostat (is regulating) the heat in this room.

3. Some burning things (produce) heat and smoke.

4. The bronchial tubes (are) inside the lungs.

Part 3

Write a word that comes from **erode** in each blank. Then fill in the circle for **verb, noun,** or **adjective.**

1. The earth loses a lot of productive land through ____erosion____ .

   ○ verb ● noun ○ adjective

2. We can't afford to let good cropland be ____eroded____ .

   ● verb ○ noun ○ adjective

3. Wind and water are ____erosive____ forces.

   ○ verb ○ noun ● adjective

4. Rain can swell rivers and ____erode____ their banks.

   ● verb ○ noun ○ adjective

Writing sentences, conventions of grammar, inflectional and derivational suffixes
Directions: If necessary, read the directions for each part. When students have completed the page, present each item and the answer. Correct any errors.

☆ Part 4

Circle the letters that should be capitalized.

1. (w)e all like the story that (j)ennifer told.

2. (m)rs. (h)icks is our neighbor and friend.

3. (j)uan and (j)anet are coming over on (s)aturday.

4. (t)he month of (n)ovember has two holidays.

5. (j)udge (k)ing said we had to finish the plan.

6. (i) wondered whether (j)essica was going to the opera.

Part 5

    fingernails   knives

1. Tell how the objects could be alike.

   (They are both sharp.)

2. Write a simile about the objects.

   (Her fingernails were like

   knives.)

      hair   cotton candy

3. Tell how the objects could be the same.

   (They are both soft and fluffy.)

4. Write a simile about the objects.

   (Her hair was like cotton candy.)

Part 6

Follow the directions.

1. Draw a vertical line.

2. Draw a line that slants up to the right from the bottom of the vertical line.

3. At the top end of the slanted line, draw a vertical line that goes down.

4. To the left of the second vertical line, write the word that means **move around.**

   circulate

Capitalization, figurative language, following directions
Directions: If necessary, read the directions for each part. When students have completed the page, present each item and the answer. Correct any errors.

184

☆ Part 1

Circle the letters that should be capital letters.

1. We went to a party for mrs. lee in november.
2. did uncle david come for thanksgiving?
3. they will go to the navesink river in september.
4. mr. casey took his class to riverside park.
5. donna took a boat ride on lake michigan last summer.
6. will grandmother come to see aunt mary?
7. mr. j. h. howard works at knollwood school.
8. the fire was at the corner of second street and main.

Part 2

Write what each analogy tells.

> What each object is made of
> Where you find each object
> What makes each object run
> What class each object is in

1. **An engine** is to gas
   as a **lightbulb** is to **electricity**.
   What makes each object run

2. **An engine** is to a car
   as a **lightbulb** is to a lamp.
   Where you find each object

3. **An engine** is to **metal**
   as a **lightbulb** is to **glass**.
   What each object is made of

Part 3

Write **R** for each fact that is **relevant** to what happened. Write **I** for each fact that is irrelevant to what happened.

> **Jimmy changed the oil in his car because it cost less than having a mechanic do it.**

1. Jimmy wears gloves. ___ I
2. Jimmy can change the oil in his car. ___ R
3. Jimmy has two dogs. ___ I
4. Jimmy wants to save money. ___ R

Part 4

Circle the subject and underline the predicate in each sentence. Rewrite each sentence by moving part of the predicate.

1. (Ducks, geese, and swans) were swimming under the dock.
   Under the dock, ducks, geese, and swans were swimming.

2. (The sixth-grade class) solved the problem without help.
   Without help, the sixth-grade class solved the problem.

3. (Blood) turns dark after its oxygen is used.
   After its oxygen is used, blood turns dark.

Part 5

Fill in each blank.

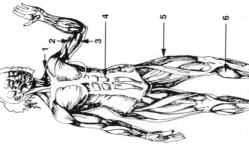

1. trapezius
2. biceps
3. triceps
4. abdominal muscle
5. quadriceps
6. gastrocnemius

Part 1

For each word on the left, write the letter of its definition on the right.

1. brain   _e_   a. (a.) that something is helpful

2. constructive   _a_   b. (n.) a wire in the body that carries messages

3. erode   _h_   c. (a.) that something is easy to predict

4. examine   _d_   d. (v.) look at

5. nerve   _b_   e. (n.) the organ that lets you think and feel

6. predictable   _c_   f. (n.) the body part that connects the brain to all parts of the body

7. spinal cord   _f_   g. (v.) use up or eat

8. consume   _g_   h. (v.) wear things down

Part 2

Complete the analogies.

1. Tell a part each object has.

A **car** is to (a steering wheel)

as a **television** is to (an antenna) .

2. Tell what each object runs on.

A **car** is to (gasoline)

as a **television** is to (electricity) .

3. Tell what class each object is in.

A **car** is to (vehicle)

as a **television** is to (appliance) .

Part 3

Label each nerve. Write a message for each nerve.

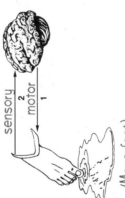

sensory
motor

1. (Move foot.)

2. (Foot feels wet.)

Definitions, analogies, graphic aids
Directions: If necessary, read the directions for each part. When students have completed the page, present each item and the answer. Correct any errors.

Part 4

Put the statements below the story in the right order.

> Rosa and Sue took their vacation in May. They packed their car with clothes and cameras, and then they started to drive to Mexico. On the way, they stopped off in Arizona. The sun was very hot, so they went swimming. They bought some rugs made by Native Americans. They ate tacos and hot chili. Then they crossed the Mexican border, and they drove toward the sea. When they found a cozy little hotel beside a sandy beach, they stopped. They stayed at the hotel for a week. They ate good Mexican food and swam in the clear, warm water every day.

They ate tacos and chili.   3

They packed their car.   1

They found a cozy little hotel.   6

They drove toward the sea.   5

They crossed the Mexican border.   4

They stopped off in Arizona.   2

Part 5

Write the conclusion to each deduction.

1. Rhonda has had some diseases.

The mumps is a disease.

So maybe Rhonda has had the mumps.

2. Commands come from the brain.

"Move leg" is a command.

So, move leg comes from the brain.

☆ Part 6

> A **homonym** is a word that sounds the same as another word, but has a different meaning and spelling.
> **Examples:** hear/here   their/there

Read each sentence. Then underline the word that completes it.

1. Bill put (some, sum) pictures on the wall.

2. The family has (bin, been) away on a trip.

3. The pitcher (through, threw) his best pitch.

4. My favorite team (won, one) the game.

5. Travis lives in a city (by, buy) the ocean.

6. Erin will (meat, meet) her brother after school.

7. Dan dug a (hole, whole) and planted the tree.

8. Could you (so, sew) this button for me?

9. Tracy's (I, eye) was swollen shut yesterday.

10. Steve grilled some (meat, meet) for our dinner.

Sequential relationships, deductions, homonyms
Directions: If necessary, read the directions for each part. When students have completed the page, present each item and the answer. Correct any errors.

186

Part 1

Answer the questions.

1. What's the rule about products that are readier to use?
   Products that are readier to
   use cost more.

2. Which costs more, a desk that is put together or a desk that comes in parts?
   A desk that is ready to use.

3. How do you know?
   It is readier to use.

Elizabeth and Jessie are both dressing up for a costume party. Jessie made her costume herself. Elizabeth's costume was already made when she bought it.

4. Whose costume costs more?
   Elizabeth's

5. How do you know?
   It is readier to use.

Part 2

Write a word that comes from **acquire** in each blank. Then fill in the circle for **verb, noun,** or **adjective.**

1 Rosa is _____ acquiring _____ a lot of money.
   ● verb   ○ noun   ○ adjective

2 How did you _____ acquire _____ that rare book?
   ● verb   ○ noun   ○ adjective

3 His coat is an expensive _____ acquisition _____ .
   ○ verb   ● noun   ○ adjective

4. Art collectors are _____ acquisitive _____ .
   ○ verb   ○ noun   ● adjective

Part 3

Cross out each wrong word and write the correct word above it. (4)

Many people don't like their jobs, but
                                          are
most firefighters is happy with their
         have
work. Most cities has a long list of
people waiting to be firefighters. If you
                                    spend
are hired as a firefighter, you must spent
several months training for the job. You
                                          must
must run, exercise, and climb ropes and
ladders. Firefighters must be very
strong because their work is very hard.

Writing sentences, inflectional and derivational suffixes, conventions of grammar
Directions: If necessary, read the directions for each part. When students have completed the page, present each item and the answer. Correct any errors.

Part 4

Put the statements below the story in the right order.

> Mike had three rabbits. He kept them in a cage. One night, the rabbits got out of the cage. They hopped under the house and wouldn't come out. Mike had to crawl under the house to grab his rabbits. He pulled them out by the ears and put them back in the cage.

The rabbits got out of the cage. __1__

Mike pulled the rabbits out by their ears. __4__

Mike put the rabbits back in the cage. __5__

The rabbits hopped under the house. __2__

Mike crawled under the house. __3__

Part 5

Shade in each tube that carries dark blood. Tell what gas each tube carries.

1. carbon dioxide
2. carbon dioxide
3. oxygen
4. oxygen

☆ Part 6

Here are some **homonyms** you know.

by	buy	A tree is by the house. Did Bob buy a new book?
hole	whole	The rabbit dug a hole. Tim ate the whole pie.
meet	meat	Meet me at six o'clock. Did dad grill the meat?
one	won	Taylor had one ticket. My cat won a red ribbon.

Read each sentence. Fill in the circle for the word that completes it.

1. My team _____ the championship.
   ○ one   ● won

2. Sally will _____ us in front of the store.
   ● meet   ○ meat

3. We ate the _____ loaf of bread.
   ○ hole   ● whole

4. Dad took me to _____ a new bike.
   ● buy   ○ by

Sequential relationships, graphic aids, homonyms
Directions: If necessary, read the directions for each part. When students have completed the page, present each item and answer. Correct any errors.

Part 1

Circle the subject and underline the predicate in each sentence. Rewrite each sentence by moving part of the predicate.

1. (Hank's mother and father) played tennis while the sun was out.

   While the sun was out, Hank's mother and father played tennis.

2. (The weather) was very dry last winter.

   Last winter, the weather was very dry.

3. (Many people) ride bikes in China.

   In China, many people ride bikes.

4. (You) must have a license to drive a car.

   To drive a car, you must have a license.

Part 2

Write **S** before each pair of **synonyms.** Write **A** before each pair of **antonyms.** Write **H** before each pair of **homonyms.**

1. __A__ more, less
2. __H__ heel, heal
3. __S__ false, untrue
4. __H__ sew, so
5. __S__ late, tardy
6. __H__ wait, weight
7. __A__ save, spend
8. __S__ neat, tidy
9. __A__ laugh, cry
10. __H__ cent, scent

Part 3

Make up a simile for each item.

1. Her eyes were very green.
   (Her eyes were like emeralds.)

2. His legs were very long.
   (His legs were like stilts.)

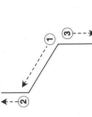

Part 4

Rewrite the paragraph in four sentences on the lines below.

> Last Monday, three men were running a race. They all had sneakers on. The man in the lead was wearing red shorts. The man in the lead had red hair. He said to himself, "If I win this race, I will get lots of money." So he ran faster. He won the race.

Last Monday, three men who were running in a race had sneakers on. The man in the lead was wearing red shorts and had red hair. He said to himself, "If I win this race, I will get lots of money." So, he ran faster and won the race.

Part 5

Write the instructions.

1. (Draw a line that slants up to the left.)

2. (Draw a vertical line up from the left end of the slanted line.)

3. (Draw a vertical line down from the right end of the slanted line.)

188

☆ Part 1

Some nouns are **irregular plurals.** Sometimes the spelling changes when a noun becomes a plural. Sometimes the spelling stays the same when the noun becomes the plural.

Singular	Plural
child	children
sheep	sheep

Fill in the circle next to the correct plural form for each noun given below.

1. deer ⚪ deers ⚫ deer
2. woman ⚪ womans ⚫ women
3. mouse ⚫ mice ⚪ mouses
4. cloth ⚫ cloth ⚪ cloths
5. goose ⚪ gooses ⚫ geese
6. shelf ⚫ shelves ⚪ shelfs
7. penny ⚪ pennys ⚫ pennies
8. tooth ⚫ teeth ⚪ tooths
9. person ⚫ people ⚪ persons
10. ox ⚪ oxes ⚫ oxen

Part 2

Write the middle part of each deduction.

1. Some rock is made of sand.
   Marble is a rock.

   So, maybe marble is made of sand.

2. Plants use carbon dioxide.
   Poison oak is a plant.

   So, poison oak uses carbon dioxide.

Part 3

Put the statements below the story in the right order.

> Marta was studying to be a doctor. In her first year of medical school, she studied the skeletal system. At the end of the year, Marta was tested on what she had learned. Marta named every bone except the upper leg bone, which she couldn't remember. She passed the test anyway, and she began studying the muscular system. In a few months, Marta could name every muscle and which bones each muscle was attached to.

_3_ Marta started studying the muscular system.

_4_ Marta could name every part of the muscular system.

_2_ Marta couldn't remember what the femur was called.

_1_ Marta started studying the skeletal system.

113

Part 4

Write a word that comes from **reside** or **acquire** in each blank. Then fill in the circle for **verb, noun,** or **adjective.**

1. She needs to __acquire__ a winter coat.

   ⚫ verb ⚪ noun ⚪ adjective

2. Many people prefer to live in __residential__ areas.

   ⚪ verb ⚪ noun ⚫ adjective

3. The __acquisition__ of diamonds is a costly hobby.

   ⚪ verb ⚫ noun ⚪ adjective

4. Jane wants to __reside__ in an apartment.

   ⚫ verb ⚪ noun ⚪ adjective

Part 5

Underline the redundant sentences.

> The salesman went from house to house, trying to get people to buy brushes. He was not selling many brushes. The man was a salesman. He had a standard sales pitch. He told people that their lives would change if they bought his brushes. Not many people fell for this pitch. The man modified his sales pitch. When he tried to sell his brushes, he gave people a different pitch.

Part 6

Fill in each blank.

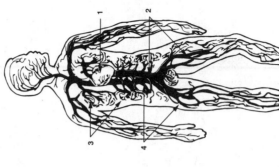

1. __heart__
2. __arteries__
3. __capillaries__
4. __veins__

Part 1

Answer the questions.

1. What's the rule about when you buy products in large quantities?
   When you buy products in large quantities, you pay less for each unit.

A man buys 10 pounds of poultry.
A supermarket buys 10,000 pounds of poultry.

2. Who buys large quantities of poultry?
   The supermarket

3. So, who pays less for each pound of poultry?
   The supermarket

4. How do you know?
   It buys in large quantities.

The store pays $60 for each suit that it buys.
Mrs. Lombardo pays $150 for each suit that she buys.

5. Who pays less for each suit?
   The store

6. So, who buys suits in large quantities?
   The store

Part 2

Write the plural form for each of the following nouns.

1. foot   feet
2. ox   oxen
3. goose   geese
4. tooth   teeth
5. man   men

Write the singular form for each of the following plural nouns.

6. women   woman
7. children   child
8. mice   mouse
9. oxen   ox
10. sheep   sheep

Writing sentences, irregular plurals
Directions: If necessary, read the directions for each part. When students have completed each page, present each item and the answer. Correct any errors.

© 2001 SRA/McGraw-Hill. Permission is granted to reproduce for classroom use.

115

Part 3

Use the facts to fill out the form.

> **Facts:** Your name is Catherine Bluefield. You are applying for a loan. You rent a house at 1255 Ackerman Road, Phoenix, Arizona, for $500 a month. You work as a legal secretary for a law firm in Phoenix called Brown and Wilson, where you make $1,300 a month. You pay about $100 a month for utilities, $250 a month for a car payment, and $50 a month for washer and dryer payments.

Instructions:

1. Name: Catherine Bluefield
2. Address: 1255 Ackerman Road, Phoenix, Arizona
3. Check one: own house ◯   rent house ●
4. Employer: Brown and Wilson
5. Position: legal secretary
6. Salary: $1,300 a month
7. Total monthly payments including rent: $900
8. Subtract line 7 from line 6: $400

Part 4

Underline the nouns. Draw a line over the adjectives. Circle the verbs.

1. Rosa and Sue (took) their vacation in May.
2. David (tried) a new plan.
3. Most people (like) sports.
4. The doctor (examined) Berta's leg.
5. Your body (uses) food and oxygen.

Part 5

Underline the redundant sentences. Cross out and correct the wording errors.

> The zoo owned a giant ape named Gog. Gog was so big that he could jump over houses and lift cars with one hand. One day, Gog broke out if his cage and started walking around the town, crushing mailboxes and fire hydrants with his feet. Gog belonged to the zoo. He saw men loading bananas onto a truck and he roared with joy. The men ran away. Gog wasn't very small, and he could lift men with a single hand. He grabbed six hundred bananas and took them back to his cage. He cage was broken.

Following instructions, conventions of grammar, writing/revising
Directions: If necessary, read the directions for each part. When students have completed each item and the answer. Correct any errors.

116   © 2001 SRA/McGraw-Hill. Permission is granted to reproduce for classroom use.

189

LESSON 59 Name _____

Part 1

For each word on the left, write the letter of its definition on the right.

1. acquire — f
2. production — l
3. criticism — j
4. demand — d
5. explanatory — k
6. erode — a
7. motor nerve — c
8. digest — e
9. sense nerve — g
10. supply — i
11. conclusion — b
12. manufactured — h

  a. (v.) wear things down
  b. (n.) the end, or something that is concluded
  c. (n.) a nerve that lets you move
  d. (n.) how well something sells
  e. (v.) change food into fuel for the body
  f. (v.) get
  g. (n.) a nerve that lets you feel
  h. (a.) that something has been made in a factory
  i. (n.) how much there is of something
  j. (n.) a statement that criticizes
  k. (a.) that something explains
  l. (n.) something that is produced

Part 2

Circle each bone that will move. Then draw an arrow that shows which way it will move.

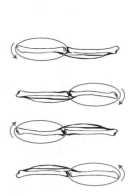

LESSON 59 Name _____

Part 3

Underline the contradiction. Circle the statement it contradicts. Tell **why** the underlined statement contradicts the circled statement. Change the underlined statement to make it true.

> The Popper Company was a large toaster manufacturer. Most of the people in Popsville worked for the Popper Company. Joyce worked for the advertising department, and she liked her job. Every day, she participated in basketball games at the factory. Besides taking part in basketball games, Joyce predicted what kind of toasters people wanted. The Popper Company always tried to make people want *more* ~~fewer~~ toasters than it could make. Joyce was very good at writing ads for the toasters.

Manufacturers try to make the demand greater than the supply.

Part 4

Read each sentence. Underline the correct form of the plural noun.

1. Are your (feet, foots) cold?
2. All the (men, mans) rode on the bus.
3. Three (womans, women) went to the picnic.
4. Terry lost two (tooths, teeth) today.
5. The three (mice, mouses) ran under the porch.

Part 5

Answer the questions.

1. What's the rule about when you buy products in large quantities?
When you buy products in large quantities, you pay less for each unit.

A supermarket buys larger quantities of meat than a person does.

2. Who pays less for meat?
A supermarket

3. How do you know?
It buys larger quantities.

Part 1

Answer the questions.

1. What's the rule about buying products in large quantities?

   When you buy products in large quantities, you pay less for each unit.

2. What's the rule about products that are readier to use?

   Products that are readier to use cost more.

Renee's Restaurant pays $6 per case of catsup.
Shopsmart pays $4 per case of catsup.

3. Who buys larger quantities of catsup?

   Shopsmart

4. Who pays less for each case of catsup?

   Shopsmart

Frank's french fries are ready to eat right away.
Frozen french fries take five minutes to fry.

5. Which french fries are readier to use?

   Frank's

6. Which french fries cost more?

   Frank's

Part 2

Fill in the circle for the word that combines the sentences correctly. Combine the sentences with that word.

1. The cat is hungry.

   The cat won't eat.

   ○ who ● however ○ particularly

   The cat is hungry; however, it won't eat.

2. The woman is swimming across the lake.

   Her son is swimming across the lake.

   ○ although ● and ○ because

   The woman and her son are swimming across the lake.

3. The femurs support the pelvis.

   The femurs are the longest bones in the body.

   ○ who ● which ○ because

   The femurs, which are the longest bones in the body, support the pelvis.

4. Wind was eroding the mountain.

   Rain was eroding the mountain.

   ○ which ○ however ● and

   Wind and rain were eroding the mountain.

Part 3

Tell which fact each statement relates to. Make each contradiction true.

1. Canned corn is readier to use than raw corn.
2. When you buy corn in large quantities, you pay less for each unit.

a. He bought cases of corn to save money.   2
b. He bought a can of corn to save time.   canned   1
c. He bought raw corn to save time.   1

Part 4

Complete the analogies.

1. Tell what part of speech each word is.

   Participatory is to adjective

   as **circulation** is to noun .

2. Tell what verb each word comes from.

   Participatory is to participate

   as **circulation** is to circulate .

3. Tell what each word means.

   Participatory is to something that involves participation

   as **circulation** is to the act of circulating .

☆ Part 5

Many words have more than one definition. For example, the word *bark* can mean "tree covering," or it can mean "the sound a dog makes."

To figure out the meaning of the word as it is used in the sentence:

• Look at the rest of the sentence.
• Decide which meaning of the word makes the most sense in the sentence.

Look at the underlined word in each sentence. Fill in the circle next to the meaning of the word that fits the sentence best.

1. Our dog needed a <u>pen</u>.

   ● fenced-in place   ○ writing tool

2. Sometimes the children argued over the <u>ball</u>.

   ● round toy that bounces   ○ a formal dance

3. On her birthday, Julie wanted a new <u>band</u> for her hair.

   ○ musicians   ● thin strip of ribbon

4. Carl placed the coins in the <u>palm</u> of my hand.

   ○ kind of tree   ● part of the hand

5. Emily looks a lot <u>like</u> her sister Laura.

   ○ to be agreeable to   ● the same or nearly the same

LESSON 61

Name _____

Part 1

Write **R** for each fact that is **relevant** to what happened. Write **I** for each fact that is **irrelevant** to what happened.

Janice went to Europe on vacation for three weeks.

1. Janice loves to travel.
2. Janice likes dogs.
3. Janice loves to visit new places.
4. Janice likes to cook.
5. Janice has two dogs and a cat.
6. Janice did not have to work at her job for three weeks.
7. Janice likes to dance.
8. Janice visited six countries in Europe.

Part 2

Write the conclusion of each deduction.

1. Things need oxygen in order to burn.

   A lighted candle is a burning thing.

   So, lighted candles need
   oxygen in order to burn.

2. Things that burn produce carbon dioxide.

   A campfire is a thing that burns.

   So, a campfire produces
   carbon dioxide.

☆ Part 3

Read the meanings in the box. Write the number of the meaning for each underlined word in the space provided.

> **light 1.** Not heavy **2.** Something by which we see
> **pound 1.** A weight equal to 16 ounces
> **2.** To hit over and over

1. __1__ He picked up a light piece of wood.
2. __2__ It weighed less than a pound.
3. __1__ Tim turned on the light so he could see.
4. __2__ She used a special tool to pound a design into the wood.

Relevant and irrelevant details, deductions, multiple meaning words
Directions: If necessary, read the directions for each part. When students have completed the page, present each item and the answer. Correct any errors.

© 2001 SRA/McGraw-Hill. Permission is granted for classroom use.

121

LESSON 61

Name _____

7. How do you know? It pays less for
   each pair.

Part 4

Answer the questions.

1. What's the rule about products that are readier to use?

   Products that are readier to
   use cost more.

2. What's the rule about buying products in large quantities?

   When you buy products in large
   quantities, you pay less for each
   unit.

   The Sporting Goods store buys larger quantities of basketball shoes than the Super-Mart store.

3. Which store pays less for basketball shoes?

   The Sporting Goods store

4. Which store probably sells basketball shoes at a lower price?

   The Sporting Goods store

   The Sporting Goods store pays $65 for each pair of basketball shoes. The Sports Spot pays $50 for each pair of basketball shoes.

5. Which store pays less for each pair of basketball shoes? The Sports Spot

6. Which store buys basketball shoes in larger quantities? The Sports Spot

Part 5

Fill in the circle for the word that combines the sentences correctly. Combine the sentences with that word.

1. The heart works all the time.
   The lungs work all the time.

   ○ especially ● and ○ although

   The heart and the lungs work
   all the time.

2. Her heart beats fast.
   Her heart beats fastest when she runs.

   ● particularly ○ although ○ and

   Her heart beats fast,
   particularly when she runs.

3. The regulation protects consumers.
   Consumers still get cheated.

   ○ which ● but ○ particularly

   The regulation protects consumers,
   but they still get cheated.

4. Robin resides in a fancy home.
   Robin acquires many expensive things.

   ● who ○ but ○ although

   Robin, who acquires many
   expensive things, resides in a
   fancy home.

Deductions, conventions of grammar
Directions: If necessary, read the directions for each part. When students have completed the page, present each item and the answer. Correct any errors.

122

© 2001 SRA/McGraw-Hill. Permission is granted to reproduce for classroom use.

☆ Part 1

Read the different meanings for each word. Write the meaning of the word as it is used in the sentence.

1. **lean:** to stand at a slant; to press against; thin

The runner was lean from so much exercise.

Meaning of **lean:** thin

Ted felt somebody lean on his shoulder.

Meaning of **lean:** to press against

2. **head:** the top part of a person's body; to be in front; a person in charge

John's dad is the head of the company.

Meaning of **head:** a person in charge

Betsy bumped her head on a branch.

Meaning of **head:** top part of a persons body

3. **trip:** a journey; to stumble and fall; to take quick steps

Jan and Tom took a trip to Ireland.

Meaning of **trip:** a journey

A crack in the sidewalk made Gina trip.

Meaning of **trip:** to stumble and fall

Part 2

Underline the nouns. Draw a line **over** the adjectives. Circle the verbs.

1. The factory is hiring fifteen new employees.
2. My sister ate many carrots and tomatoes for dinner.
3. Many birds fly to Florida every winter.
4. Her father explained his criticism of the new regulations.
5. Her boss runs six miles every day.

Part 3

Make each statement mean the same thing as the statement in the box.

> **Although every person produces carbon dioxide, there is not much in the air.**

1. All people produce carbon dioxide, but there is not much in the air.
2. Although people use up carbon dioxide, there isn't a lot in the air.   *produce*
3. Every person makes carbon dioxide, but there's a lot in the air.   *produces*   *not much*
4. Every person consumes carbon dioxide; however, there is not much in the air.   *produces*

123

Part 4

Rewrite the story in six sentences on the lines below.

> One day, Ellen fell down the stairs and hurt one of the nerves in her spinal cord. She broke three ribs, and the doctor said that Ellen would have to stay in bed for a long time. He told her that she had hurt a nerve in her central nervous system and he said that she had broken a part of her skeletal system.

One day, Ellen fell down the stairs. Ellen hurt one of the nerves in her spinal cord. She broke three ribs. The doctor said that Ellen would have to stay in bed for a long time. He told her that she had hurt a nerve in her central nervous system. He said that she had broken a part of her skeletal system.

Part 5

Write the instructions.

①   │ ② unfortunate
     │ ③

1. (Draw a vertical line.)
2. (Write the word unfortunate to the right of the line.)
3. (Draw a horizontal line over the word unfortunate.)

Part 6

Fill in each blank with the word that has the same meaning as the word or words under the blank.

1. Sarah felt unlucky when she lost the card game. (not lucky)
2. Not wearing a bicycle helmet is unintelligent. (not smart)
3. I modified my bike last summer. (changed)
4. I failed the test because I was unprepared. (not prepared)
5. Digestion begins after eating. (act of digesting)

124

LESSON 63

Name _____

Part 1

Put the statements below the story in the right order.

> Claire had just finished high school, and she wanted to make a lot of money. Because so many people ride bikes, she decided to start making bicycle seats. She made 1,000 seats, but nobody wanted them. Claire tried to think of ways to sell the seats. She put ads on television that told how comfortable the seats were. Then she offered a free pen with every seat. Pretty soon, she had to lower her prices. She started to think that making seats wasn't such a good idea after all.

_4_ She puts ads on television.

_1_ Claire finished high school.

_3_ She made 1,000 bicycle seats.

_5_ She offered a free pen with every seat.

_2_ She decided to make bicycle seats.

_6_ She lowered her prices.

Part 2

Fill in the circle for the word that combines the sentences correctly. Combine the sentences with that word.

1. Lynn and her sister met for lunch.

   Lynn and her sister met to go shopping.

   ○ because ○ especially ● and

   Lynn and her sister met for lunch and to go shopping.

2. Mrs. Ferguson is very wealthy.

   Mrs. Ferguson owns the local newspaper.

   ○ however ● who ○ although

   Mrs. Ferguson, who owns the local newspaper, is very wealthy.

3. Melissa consumed lots of food.

   She did not feel full.

   ● although ○ which ○ and

   Although Melissa consumed lots of food, she did not feel full.

LESSON 63

Name _____

Part 3

Make up a simile for each item.

1. The school bus was very slow.

   (The school bus was like a turtle.)

2. The woman in the pool swam very gracefully.

   (The woman in the pool swam like a swan.)

3. Her fingernails were long and sharp.

   (Her fingernails were like claws.)

Part 4

Make each statement mean the same thing as the statement in the box.

> That factory regulates its production daily.

1. That factory controls its production every day.
   regulated

2. What that factory makes is criticized daily.
   production

3. That factory controls its selection every day.

4. What that factory makes is regulated daily.

☆ Part 5

- To make a **singular noun** show ownership, add an **apostrophe** and **s ('s)**.

  The girl's bike is red.

- To make a plural noun show ownership, add an **apostrophe after the s (s')**.

  The two girls' bicycles were in the yard.

- If a plural noun does not end with s, add an **apostrophe** and **s ('s)**.

  The women's club meets on Thursday.

Write the possessive form of each noun.

1. cousin   cousin's

2. teacher   teacher's

3. brother   brother's

4. workers   workers'

5. kitten   kitten's

6. boys   boys'

7. school   school's

8. planes   planes'

9. dinosaur   dinosaur's

10. doctors   doctors'

Name _____

Part 1

For each word on the left, write the letter of its definition on the right.

1. acquire	f	a. (a.) that something protects
2. circulation	g	b. (a.) smart
3. fortunate	i	c. (a.) not lucky
4. intelligent	b	d. (n.) the act of respiring
5. protective	a	e. (v.) live somewhere
6. redundant	k	f. (v.) get
7. regulate	l	g. (n.) the act of circulating
8. reside	e	h. (a.) not smart
9. unfortunate	c	i. (a.) lucky
10. respiration	d	j. (a.) that someone or something is careful about selecting things
11. unintelligent	h	k. (a.) that something repeats what has already been said
12. selective	j	l. (v.) control

Part 2

Follow the directions.

1. Print the adjective that means **that someone or something is careful about selecting things.**

2. Draw a vertical line to the left of the word.

3. Draw a horizontal line under the word.

4. Under the horizontal line, print the noun that means **the act of circulating.**

| selective
_____
circulation

Definitions, following directions
Directions: If necessary, read the directions for each part. When students have completed the page, present each item and the answer. Correct any errors.

Name _____

☆ Part 3

Rewrite each phrase to show ownership. Add an **apostrophe** or an **apostrophe and -s** to the underlined words.

1. a clown hat — a clown's hat
2. a snowman nose — a snowman's nose
3. five dogs bones — five dogs' bones
4. the pilots hats — the pilots' hats
5. six kites strings — six kites' strings
6. the children presents — the children's presents
7. the cats toys — the cats' toys
8. the neighbors lawn — the neighbor's lawn
9. the sisters farm — the sisters' farm
10. the oxen hooves — the oxen's hooves

Part 4

Put the statements below the story in the right order.

> Matthew wanted to throw a surprise party for his mom's fiftieth birthday. First, he decided when to have the party. He picked Friday night. Then, he bought the invitations and sent them in the mail. He bought streamers and balloons to decorate the house. The next day he bought food for the party and the birthday cake. On the night of the party, he had his dad take his mom shopping while the guests secretly arrived. Once everyone was there, it was safe for Matthew's dad to bring his mom home. When she walked into the kitchen and turned on the light, everyone yelled, "Surprise!" Matthew's mother talked and danced all night long.

The guests at the party yelled, "Surprise!"   6
Matthew decided on a date.   1
Matthew's dad took his mom shopping.   5
Matthew bought food for the party.   4
Matthew sent out invitations.   2
Matthew bought streamers and balloons.   3

Possessive nouns, sequential relationships
Directions: If necessary, read the directions for each part. When students have completed the page, present each item and the answer. Correct any errors.

195

196

Part 1

Follow the directions.

1. Draw a horizontal line.

2. From the right end of the horizontal line, draw a long slanted line up to the left.

3. At the top end of the slanted line, draw a vertical line down through the horizontal line.

4. In the triangle, write the noun that means **something you get.**

acquisiton

Part 2

smile   sunshine

1. Tell how the objects could be alike.
(They could both be bright.)

2. Write a simile about the objects.
(Her smile was like sunshine.)

3. Tell how the objects are not alike.
(Her smile is not hot.)

☆ Part 3

Write the possessive noun that goes with each phrase.

1. the petals on the flower
the flower's petal

2. the aunt of the girl
the girl's aunt

3. the mother of the twins
the twins' aunt

4. the videos of the boy
the boy's videos

Write what each possessive noun means.

1. the sheep's wool
the wool of the sheep

2. the book's cover
the cover of the book

3. the boy's friends
the friends of the boy

4. the sun's warmth
the warmth of the sun

Part 4

Fill in each blank with the word that has the same meaning as the word or words under the blank.

1. It was very ___unfortunate___ that it
(not lucky)
stormed the day of the party.

2. Sheila had to ___rearrange___ the pile of
(put in order again)
papers after she dropped them.

3. Janet was ___unprepared___ when the
(not prepared)
unexpected guests showed up for dinner.

4. It is ___unbelievable___ that it can be
(not believable)
seventy degrees one day and thirty degrees the next day.

5. When her boss offered her more money, Debbie ___reconsidered___ leaving
(thought about again)
the company.

6. Marni said that she wanted to ___redo___
(do again)
the math problems.

Part 5

Answer the questions.

1. What's the rule about what manufacturers try to do?
Manufacturers try to make the demand greater than the supply.

The Barbecue Manufacturing Company makes 1500 grills a week. People buy 800 grills a week.

2. Which is greater, the supply or the demand?
The supply

3. What will happen to the price of barbecue grills?
It will go down.

4. What will the Barbecue Manufacturing Company try to do? They will try to make the demand greater than the supply.

Name two ways that the Barbecue Manufacturing Company can do that.

5. Advertise the grills

6. Put extras on the grills